Maximum Tennis

10 Keys to Unleashing Your On-Court Potential

Nick Saviano

Human Kinetics

Library of Congress Cataloging-in-Publication Data

Saviano, Nick, 1955-
  Maximum tennis : 10 keys to unleashing your on-court potential / Nick
Saviano
     p. cm
   ISBN: 0-7360-4200-8 (soft cover)
  1. Tennis   I. Title.
   GV995 .S28 2002
   796.352--dc21

                                                        2002005930

ISBN: 0-7360-4200-8

Acquisitions Editor: Martin Barnard; **Managing Editor:** Wendy McLaughlin; **Assistant Editors:** Kim Thoren; Dan Brachtesende; **Copyeditor:** Erin Cler; **Proofreader:** Pam Johnson; **Indexer:** Joan Griffitts; **Permission Manager:** Toni Harte; **Graphic Designer:** Robert Reuther; **Art and Photo Managers:** Dan Wendt; Carl Johnson; **Cover Designer:** Keith Blomberg; **Photographer (cover):** © Lance Jeffrey; **Illustrator:** Michael Greenberg; **Printer:** Versa Press

Printed in the United States of America 10 9 8 7 6 5 4 3 2 1

Human Kinetics
Web site: www.HumanKinetics.com

United States: Human Kinetics
P.O. Box 5076
Champaign, IL 61825-5076
800-747-4457
e-mail: humank@hkusa.com

Canada: Human Kinetics
475 Devonshire Road Unit 100
Windsor, ON N8Y 2L5
800-465-7301 (in Canada only)
e-mail: orders@hkcanada.com

Europe: Human Kinetics
107 Bradford Road
Stanningley
Leeds LS28 6AT, United Kingdom
+44 (0) 113 255 5665
e-mail: hk@hkeurope.com

Australia: Human Kinetics
57A Price Avenue
Lower Mitcham, South Australia 5062
08 8277 1555
e-mail: liahka@senet.com.au

New Zealand: Human Kinetics
P.O. Box 105-231, Auckland Central
09-523-3462
e-mail: hkp@ihug.co.nz

To my beautiful family—my wife, Jenny, and my daughters Nicole, Amanda, and Jennifer.

Contents

Chapter 1   Visualize Your Ultimate Player   1

The path to success is a developmental plan that evolves from a vision of the player you want to be. You have to see it in order to get there.

Jim Courier—Know where you need to go.

Chapter 2   Embrace Your Playing Personality   19

Your on-court instincts should be the driving force in developing a playing style and formulating match strategy.

Chris Evert—Bring "you" into your game.

Chapter 3   Customize Tactics   41

In the heat of the battle, stay on track by focusing on shots and tactical adjustments that reinforce your overall match strategy.

Nick Bollettieri—Know your strategy and adjust your tactics.

Chapter 4   Optimize Technique   67

Focusing on the true fundamentals of technique will allow your natural hitting style to emerge, enabling you to hit cleanly, consistently, and with power.

Patrick McEnroe—Play your best weapon.

Chapter 5 Let Movement Flow   93

Efficient movement has as much to do with the right mental approach as it does with technique. Use your subconscious mind to make court movement automatic.

Dennis Van der Meer—Make your movements an instinct!

Chapter 6 Simulate for Success   115

Re-create match conditions in practice to prepare for every physical and mental challenge your opponents can throw at you.

Brad Gilbert—Practice with purpose.

Chapter 7 Focus On What You Can Control   129

Everyone faces mental challenges on the court. The key to overcoming them is to zero in on what is within your ability and ignore the rest.

Dick Gould—Work at having a winning mentality.

Chapter 8 Guarantee Success   145

Winning and losing don't always define success. Through preparation, long-term planning, and evaluation, you can improve with every match.

Stan Smith—Being prepared is half the battle.

Chapter 9 Synergize in Doubles   159

Make a successful transition from singles to doubles by creating synergism in communication, movement, positioning, and strategy.

Pam Shriver—Pick a good partner and play off each other's strengths.

Chapter 10 Play From the Heart   173

Fun and enjoyment of the game are the foundation from which everything grows. Follow these steps to free your game to reach its potential.

Billie Jean King—Play for the fun of it!

Foreword

Players have a lot of options to turn to for tennis instruction these days in magazines, books, and on the Internet. And believe me, I have seen plenty of books come across my desk since becoming publisher of *TENNIS* magazine. From stroke instruction, to mental training, to physical conditioning, they cover just about every possible aspect of becoming a better player.

So what's different about this book? Plenty. It is the only book I've seen that lays out all the intangibles that will help you play to your full potential. And like a good approach shot, this book has real depth. If tennis was as simple as working on your serve or your forehand, the world would be filled with great players. But it's much more than that. It's your attitude, your frame of reference, and how you approach technique, tactics, and even practice. Many players suffer by practicing the wrong thing.

It's no coincidence that some of the game's best players and coaches agree. Thumb through the chapters and you'll see how they identify with Nick's concepts at the beginning of each chapter. You'll find entertaining stories with the underlying message that these players became great because they learned these principles, often the hard way. From years of playing and coaching at game's highest levels, Nick has captured these concepts in one book, so you can get on the right track faster. I've known Nick for over 25 years. We have had the opportunity to work with players together on court and time and time again he has shown excellent insight and vision as to what the player needs to do to reach their full potential. The bottom line is this: his approach works.

No matter how you play, or what level you are starting from, you'll be a better player for reading this book. That's what the "maximum" in *Maximum Tennis* means—you'll get the absolute most out of your ability to play. And win or lose, you'll enjoy the journey!

Chris Evert

Acknowledgments

To my mom, Carmella, and my dad, Dominick (who is deceased) for their unconditional support, encouragement and love, as well as my eight brothers and sisters.

To Father Joe Dispenza, PhD, who passed away in 1992, and helped shape my basic philosophy not only on the psychology of sport but about life as well. Many of the concepts I write about in chapter 7 are a direct result of his influence.

Rainer Martens, PhD, who pointed me in the right direction with this book, provided excellent guidance, and then gave me the opportunity to write my first book. To Martin Barnard and Wendy McLaughlin for their professionalism, work ethic, and guidance in getting this project accomplished.

A special thanks within the USTA family to Paul Roetert, PhD, and Paul Lubbers, PhD, for reviewing the book and offering suggestion and guidance along the way; and, to Ron Woods, PhD, for years of help in refining my skills in the field of coaching education.

To Jon Levey for reviewing the book and helping with the introductions for the chapters.

Special thanks to Chris Evert for writing the foreword and for totally supporting my efforts in this project.

To the ten world-class experts: Nick Bollettieri, Jim Courier, Chris Evert, Brad Gilbert, Dick Gould, Billie Jean King, Pat McEnroe, Pam Shriver, Stan Smith, and Dennis Van der Meer, for giving up their valuable time to write an introduction for their chapter.

To Dick Gould who gave me my first tennis lesson at 12 years old and has never stopped teaching me since. Thanks for your friendship, support, and guidance for over 35 years.

To Nick Bollettieri and Dennis Van der Meer—two coaching legends that have openly shared their wisdom and tennis knowledge with me.

To the hundreds, if not thousands, of players I have had the opportunity to work with. You have educated me far more than I have taught you.

Finally, to all the thousands of coaches around the country that I have had the privilege to work and interact with. You put your heart and soul into developing players and rarely get the credit you deserve. I appreciate and respect you more than you will ever know.

Introduction

If you have a passion for the game of tennis you've probably tried just about everything to make your game better. I've been down the same road. It took me 35 years as a junior player, a pro on the ATP Tour, a professional coach, and a director of coaching education to finally figure out what it is that allows players to reach their full potential. I call them the real truths, or the key fundamentals of the game. These fundamentals are executed by the truly great players like Andre Agassi, Venus and Serena Williams, Pete Sampras, Jennifer Capriati, Lleyton Hewitt, and other tennis professionals. They are the common denominators that transcend all styles of play and bring success at every level of the game!

Each chapter presents one of these 10 key fundamentals. Some of the best players and coaches introduce each chapter, giving you an idea how they used these concepts to raise the level of their own games or the level of their players. The key fundamentals cover all facets of the game, from chapter 1 on how to set up a developmental plan and chapter 4 optimizing technique, to chapter 10 on the critical importance of having fun, enjoyment and cultivating a passion for the game. In my mind, one of the biggest keys to success is having fun and chapter 10 will give you insights into what you can do to enhance the positives and erase the negatives from your game.

Whether you're hoping to reach the upper echelons of competitive tennis, are a club player attempting to win the club championship at your rating level, or a coach who is looking for new insight into developing players, this book will help you not only reach your goals but break through them. Read on, and here's to reaching your maximum tennis potential!

CHAPTER 1

Visualize Your Ultimate Player

> "The path to success is a developmental plan that evolves from a vision of the player you want to be. You have to see it in order to get there."

Establishing a developmental plan is the key to taking your game to the next level or even reaching your full potential as a player if you are really serious. It is in essence a blueprint for your development and creates what I call "systematic training." It spells out precisely what you need to work on in all aspects of your game, and it details the way that development should be accomplished. It will provide clarity and focus not only for you but for your coach, as well. And believe me, it will be a tremendous source of motivation and inspiration on a daily basis.

Jim Courier

4-time Grand Slam Champion and former No. 1 in the world

This chapter really hits the bull's eye with the concept of a developmental plan. Reaching your full potential as a tennis player is a journey. It doesn't happen after a few lessons and there aren't any shortcuts. Anytime you embark on that kind of voyage of discovery, if you want to reach your destination, it's wise to have a detailed map as your guide. You need a definitive plan that navigates your development through all the possibilities you have as a player. Whether you're someone hoping to capture the 4.0 championship at your club or hoisting the U.S. Open trophy, the means are still the same. You have to establish clearly defined terms of how you want to accomplish this goal. Too many players allow their games to futilely wander, hoping to miraculously find the secret ingredient to success. Take it from me, it doesn't happen that way. Not in tennis. You need to create the road map that will take you there. And that's the purpose of this important opening chapter. It will get your game pointed firmly in the right direction.

This chapter will help you design a developmental plan that sets up your goals and find clear paths for achieving them. After you make progress on your journey, and that map becomes dated, you must re-evaluate your goals and construct a new plan.

As a player, I was constantly determining what my strengths and weaknesses were physically, mentally, emotionally, and technically. I went about figuring ways to better my weaknesses and solidify my strengths. I was very diligent about covering all the parts of my game. The ideas for improvement came naturally to me while I was a junior battling my peers at Nick Bollettieri's Academy and with the U.S. Junior Davis Cup Team. That intense, competitive environment spurred me to look for avenues to raise the level of my game. I was fortunate to have some great coaches help me with my path so I never veered too far off course. By age 14 or 15, I was committed to working on whatever it took to see what I could ultimately be as a player.

The best feeling anybody can have is knowing that there's no doubt you've achieved your maximum potential. It takes a tremendous amount of hard work and it doesn't come easy. But it's a journey that's truly worth taking. Read this chapter carefully, develop a plan that's right for you, work hard, and learn what it takes to reach your full potential.

Establishing a Developmental Plan

The first and most important step in your personal improvement is the principle I call "planning from the inside out." I started refining this concept after reading Stephen Covey's book *The Seven Habits of Highly Effective People*, in which he talks about the inside-out approach to personal and interpersonal effectiveness.

What do I mean by planning from the inside out? I mean that you begin by reflecting on and then creating your personal vision of the ultimate player you want to become. This is the critical component to the success of the entire developmental plan. Your vision provides clarity and focus. It provides positive motivation rather than negative criticism. You will be able to recognize exactly what you need to do with your game, why it is important, and what level of priority you should give it in your overall scheme. Your vision also creates a link between your daily training and the ultimate player you want to become. Without this type of plan that starts from the inside out, you are engaging in "random training," which is a hit-and-miss approach to practice. It is an extremely inefficient and often ineffective way to practice or develop your game. You may work hard on your tennis yet have virtually nothing to show for it. Talk about frustration!

Several years ago, a young touring professional, Vince Spadea, and his father approached me for some guidance regarding Vince's tennis development. I had known Vince since he was 15 years old and had spent time with him on the United States Tennis Association (USTA) national team for four years. He had been one of the top juniors in the world and was an extremely talented player. Vince was struggling with his confidence. His results were subpar, and his world ranking had stagnated in the 300s. I invited Vince and his father to my office to discuss his situation and to give him a sense of direction.

I explained to them that, despite all his hard work, Vince needed a focused plan to help him develop to his potential. They agreed, and we started putting together a comprehensive developmental plan. Planning from the inside out, Vince talked about where his game was at the time and what his personal vision was of the ultimate player he wanted to become. As he

Children younger than 14 years old don't need to go through the entire process. They will benefit from discussions on the vision of the kind of player they want to become and on what they need to develop in their game. But because they are still learning the basic fundamentals of technique, tactics, and rules of the game, a full-fledged developmental plan is premature. You need to plan with your child's coach—even if the child is not directly involved at this stage.

Vince Spadea and Nick Saviano after Spadea's win at the 1992 18s Orange Bowl.

spoke, I provided feedback to make sure that his vision reflected his personality, physical skills, and how he loved to play. This was the key to the success of the whole process because, as he crystallized his vision, the other areas of his game that he needed to address would start to fall into place. A logical progression began to develop. After the vision, Vince began to see the game strategies, tactics, and techniques he needed to address; the psychological areas he needed to strengthen; the physical conditioning he needed to work on; and the scheduling considerations he needed to make. Finally, we set specific goals to accomplish those objectives.

The whole process only took about two hours. Obviously, Vince's plan was far more in depth and took more time than a plan for the average competitive player. You can actually do a "turbocharged" developmental plan—believe it or not—in about 15 minutes and cover enough ground to give you the same basic benefits. However, the more serious you are about your game, the more detailed and in depth you will want your plan to be.

At the end of our meeting, I could see that Vince was more at peace about his future, while at the same time he was really fired up and ready to go. I told him and his father before they left that, if he followed his plan, he could break into the top 100 on the Association of Tennis Professionals (ATP) world rankings within a year.

We stayed in touch throughout the next year. Vince followed the principles that we had laid out in the plan, and we made adjustments to it, as required, as his game evolved. The results were surprising. Vince won three challenger events (the "minor" leagues of professional tennis) and then started beating some of the top world-class players on the tour. His world ranking skyrocketed from the 300s to the top 60 in less than eight months.

Most of all, Vince's improvement was a credit to his talent, his work ethic, his commitment to tennis, and his family's support. But it was the developmental plan that provided Vince with clear, unambiguous guidance to maximize his efforts. Over the next few years, Vince continued to improve and worked his way up to the top 20 in the world, and he was named to the U.S. Davis Cup team.

Vince Spadea's situation is not an isolated case. I have used the concept of establishing a developmental plan for the past 10 years and have had great success with players at all levels of the game.

You can establish a sound developmental plan in less than 30 minutes, but you will need help from someone who either knows your game well or from a certified U.S. Professional Tennis Association (USPTA) or Professional Tennis Registry (PTR) professional. You should also periodically update and refine your plan. As you read about the different components to the developmental plan, don't be intimidated. Even if you simply go through the process in your mind without even writing anything down, it will help you to clarify what and how you need to proceed with your development. Regardless of the time you commit to it, 15 minutes or two hours, the results can be profound.

Developmental Team Leader

Each player should have a designated developmental team leader (DTL). This person is responsible for taking the lead role in guiding your development. Your DTL can be your coach or a parent; or, if you are an adult, you can be your own DTL. The more serious you are, the more you will need an expert to help you set up and execute your plan. The DTL's role is to help keep you on track and to make sure that you are getting everything you need to reach your goals.

The input from your DTL will include hands-on coaching, on and off the court (in some cases the DTL will not do any actual coaching), and monitoring all the other information, tips, instruction, or advice that is passed on to you to be sure that it fits into your systematic training objectives. In other words, you'll hear a lot of stuff about tennis that may not always be accurate or right for you, and you don't want conflicting advice or information that is not consistent with your plan. At the world-class level, virtually every top player during the past 15 to 20 years has had one key person taking on this role (for example, Venus and Serena Williams—their father; Andre Agassi—his former coach, Brad Gilbert; Martina Hingis—her mother; Jim Courier—Jose Higueras; Jennifer Capriati—her father, Stefano; Lindsay Davenport—her coach, Robert Van't Hof). The same holds true for top juniors, as well. The DTL is probably the most significant common denominator among the top players in the game today.

Current Personal Assessment

To get where you want to go with your game, you need to know where you are now. A realistic assessment of your current game is a *must*. Your DTL can be a great help here because it is difficult to be accurate or, in some cases, realistic about your own skill level.

You need to review what style of game you play, whether that style is the right one for you, and what your strengths and weaknesses are in the various aspects of the game. You can do this in a few minutes' time. Once you know where you are, you can think about where you want to go.

Long-Term Vision

What kind of player do you want to be? Do you have ambitions of being world-class or just an all-around great weekend player? Whatever your goal, you need to develop a vivid vision of the player you ultimately want to become. This will be the backbone and guiding light of your plan. You need to take into consideration your personality and how you like to play. As you reflect, try to imagine all aspects of your game. How will you play under pressure? What weapons will you have? What style of game will you play?

Your vision should maximize your strengths and minimize your weaknesses. If you are short, don't have a big serve, and hate to play the net, don't envision yourself becoming another Pete Sampras. If you are tall and slow, chances are you'll never become another Serena Williams. Be realistic in your assessment, but, most important of all, your vision should excite and motivate you.

Remember, you are unique, as a person and a player, and your vision should reflect that. You need to develop the player *you* can be, not anyone else's potential. Besides being based on your dreams, your vision should also take into consideration commitment levels and time constraints. For example, if you are a 50-year-old who can play only three hours a week on the weekend, your vision is going to be totally different from that of a 13-year-old tournament-playing junior who wants to become a world-class player. Keep in mind, however, that the same principles apply.

Strategy and Game Style

Once you have a clear vision of the player you want to become, you need to establish the appropriate game style and strategy to help make that vision a reality. Discuss with your DTL what strategy and patterns need to be mastered and the weapons you need to develop to achieve your objective. Before you do this, I recommend you read chapter 2, to help you clarify exactly how to set up the right game style and strategy for you.

I met Stefano Capriati when his daughter was playing in the prestigious Easter Bowl Junior event in the girls' 16-and-under. I was a national coach at the time. He told me about his vision of the type of player his daughter Jennifer would be: athletic, strong, and hard hitting with a big serve. It was apparent to me that Stefano had a definite plan for Jennifer's development. I had met a lot of parents with high hopes for their child's tennis but not many with this type of clarity for the future. His daughter was already outstanding. She got to the quarterfinals that year, which of itself was not so extraordinary until you take into account that she was only ten years old! But it wasn't until four years later—in a cold, soggy, dimly lit, leaky-roofed, bumpy, indoor clay court on a cold, rainy Sunday in Charleroi, Belgium—that I saw Stefano's vision becoming a reality. It was there that I watched Jennifer Capriati win her first International Tennis Federation (ITF) 18-and-under. One week later, she won the French Junior championships at the age of 13. And, although it has not always been smooth sailing through all of the ups and downs over the years, Stefano's vision (which he instilled in Jennifer) of the great player Jennifer could be never seemed to waver and ultimately became a reality.

Lynne Rolley, Jennifer and Stefano Capriati, and Nick Saviano after Jennifer's win in her first International Tennis Federation 18s and under junior event in Charleroi, Belgium.

Tactical Considerations

The best advice I can give you is this—watch the pros. The best players consistently make good tactical decisions in the heat of battle, and those decisions are almost always within the context of their overall strategy.

Tactical discussions should follow talks of strategy development. If you focus on tactical adjustments without a clearly defined strategy, it will lead to a lack of direction and purpose when competing. Determine what key tactical skills (aside from the standard tactical principles) you need to develop that are most important for your particular strategy. For example, if you are an aggressive ground stroker with a big forehand and a weak backhand, the forehand inside-out pattern is important for you. Or, if you like to play the net, you must use various ways of tactically adjusting (such as coming in behind a second serve). Chapter 3 goes into more detail about how you can use tactics to improve your strategy in a way that works for you.

Technical Development

Most players, when they think of improving their game, jump right into tinkering with the mechanics of their strokes. Sometimes that causes more problems than it solves. Only after you have established a well-defined vision, strategy, and tactical plan can you efficiently discuss what you need to work on technically. It's not only important to know what to work on, but it's just as important to know how to prioritize those needs and how much time to spend on each. Changing mechanics or tweaking your strokes can be difficult and frustrating, but, when it is part of a master plan, you will understand why it needs to be done and you'll have the intrinsic motivation to see it through. For a more detailed look at technique, see chapter 4.

Psychological Development

This component of your developmental plan is part of mastering your mind. Think about how you will compete and how to psychologically conduct yourself before, during, and after competition. After determining what psychological skills you need to develop or improve, establish a simple plan that allows you to take modest steps forward. In chapter 7, "Focus on What You Can Control," I discuss some of the psychological secrets of the pros that will provide you with information to help you get on the right track.

Scheduling and Periodization

Put together a tournament/match schedule that will enable you to maximize your results and allow for adequate rest and recovery. To do this you need to understand basic concepts of scheduling and periodization. Athletes, especially tennis players, cannot play at their absolute best every day, all year long. Your body and mind need time to rest and recover after exerting maximum effort. World-class athletes have learned how to practice and compete to peak at certain times of the year. That is called periodization.

You can use these principles to target when you want to be at your best, then set up a program of practice and competition that will put you there. Discuss with your DTL how many total tournaments you should play during the year, the optimum number of tournaments in a row, the amount of practice you need between competitions, and the rest time required for maximum benefit. For example, when I was on the pro tour, I liked to play up to 30 tournaments a year—which is a lot for a professional—and I scheduled myself to play 4 or 5 tournaments in a row. That is what worked best for me. However, other professionals, such as Bjorn Borg or Jimmy Connors, played as few as 15 tournaments per year and would schedule only two events in a row (they were also winning or getting to the finals of most of the events they played). You may simply have one club match a week or one tournament a month. My point is that everyone is different. Do what works best for you.

Physical Development

No plan is complete without an examination of the physical side of the game. At this stage you will assess what you need to do physically to reach your goals. Do you need to get stronger? Increase your aerobic base? Work on your speed or footwork? Even if you are not that serious as a player, by understanding what you need to work on and implementing the most basic plan, you can have a significant impact on your results. Let's say you get winded too easily after a long point and you always lose the next two because you are tired. Simply adding a few drills at the end of practice to get your heart rate up can help significantly. Chapter 6 discusses specific ways to practice that may help you out.

Goal Setting

Finally, you need to set up goals to accomplish your objectives. Once again, these can be incredibly simple and basic, or they can be more comprehensive, which would include short-term, intermediate, and long-term performance goals. But make no mistake, having goals will make it easier to maintain motivation and endure the necessary sacrifices to reach the ultimate outcome.

Brian Dunn was 16 years old when he was named a member of the U.S. national team. Brian made it clear to me that he wanted to become a world-class professional. He was an excellent student (both his mother and father were professors at a university) as well as one of the top juniors in the country, and was being coached by his father. He was willing to forgo college if his potential warranted it. However, the family was concerned about the enormous cost of starting out playing the professional circuit.

To address the issue, we set up a developmental plan to help Brian not only improve his game but set himself up as one of the world's top prospects to attract significant endorsement contracts to pay his way into the pros. His specific "outcome goals" (outcome goals will be discussed in detail in chapter 7) were to win the 18 Nationals, the U.S. Open Junior title, and to finish the year as the number one–ranked junior in the world. Very high goals indeed!

Nick Saviano and Brian Dunn at the 1992 Junior U.S. Open. Brian finished as the No. 1 junior in the world.

With the support of his parents, we mapped out a clear long-range vision and developmental plan for his game. It was not an easy road! There were many ups and downs, particularly in his first year in the 18-and-under juniors. But step by step, Brian continued to improve. As he entered his last year of junior competition, his game started to evolve. He reached the final of the Australian Juniors, though he played poorly in the title match. He had a quarterfinal showing at the Italian Juniors, followed by a disappointing loss early at the French. This was a particularly big setback because he was one of the favorites and many sports agents and company representatives came out to watch him play. Brian rebounded by winning the warm-up event before Wimbledon and then reaching the final of the Wimbledon Juniors (though again, he had a disappointing loss in the final). He stuck to his plan, however, and continued to work hard as we made subtle refinements as his game evolved. His focus now turned to the U.S. National Junior championships at Kalamazoo, Michigan, the winner of which receives a direct entry into the men's event at the U.S. Open. It took five grueling sets, but Brian won the title.

The stage was now set for Brian. If he could have a good showing against a top player in the main draw of the U.S. Open and do well in the Junior Open, he could solidify the number-one world junior ranking and possibly earn an endorsement contract that would enable him to pursue his professional dream. Brian came through with flying colors. In the first round, he beat a player from Germany who was ranked in the top 100 of the ATP world rankings, then lost in the second round after playing an excellent match. He followed up that performance by winning the U.S. Open Junior title and sewed up the number-one ranking in the world. Brian then turned pro and signed lucrative endorsement contracts.

But that is not the end of the story. Brian was besieged with knee injuries during the first 18 months of his pro career. Two operations subsequently put an end to his career before it ever had a chance to take off. Brian went back to school, earned a college degree, and went on to get his law degree from Georgetown University.

Two years ago I received a call from Brian. He was planning to get married and was excited about his career in law. During the conversation, he told me, "Nick, I wanted to thank you because many of the principles you spoke about—having a clear vision and setting up a plan—are principles I have used as I pursued my law degree. They have really helped me to accomplish my goals and make my vision a reality." His comments meant as much to me as any others I have received in tennis. His words solidified my belief in the benefits and importance of planning from the inside out and establishing a clear developmental plan.

This chapter may seem to present a lot of information to be assimilated all at once, but don't be intimidated. Once you understand the process of planning from the inside out, your developmental plan can be completed in less than 30 minutes.

I've also included examples of two detailed developmental plans. The first is for a 45-year-old, male recreational player who is rated 4.0 on the National Tennis Rating Program (NTRP) scale. His goal is to reach the 4.5 level. His plan would normally take about 45 minutes to put together. The second plan is for a 13-year-old girl who has aspirations of becoming a world-class player. This plan would take significant discussion to set up. Plan on a couple of hours to develop such a program.

Look at the two sample developmental programs (forms 1.1 and 1.2). It is clear that the same basic principles work for the serious player, as well as the social player.

Don't drop this book and attempt to set up a complete plan right now. As you read through the rest of the book, many things about the game in general and your game in particular will become clearer to you. You'll have a better understanding of the process, of your game, and where you want to go with it. One thing is certain: If you take the time to establish even a modest plan and you are willing to work at it, your chances of taking your game to the next level are pretty darn good!

DEVELOPMENTAL PLAN I
For the Serious Recreational Player

PLAYER: "John Smith"
PLAYER DESCRIPTION: Male, 45 years old, 6'1"
DEVELOPMENTAL TEAM LEADER: Coach's Name (USPTA or PTR Certified)

PLAYER EVALUATION
- Playing at the 4.0 level.
- Game style: Net rusher
- Serve is steady and consistent.
- Volleys are consistent but doesn't put them away well.
- Ground strokes are consistent, but backhand is a little weak. Approach shots are good.
- Mentally strong and competes well.

[Note: Most people would think that John should spend a lot of time on improving his backhand. But as we've seen, that is not necessarily the right plan.]

LONG-TERM VISION
I love attacking the net, serving and volleying, and hitting approach shots so I can come in behind them. I have a big serve and win a lot of free points with it. My serve also sets me up for easy volleys. I am very good at the net—a consistent volleyer with the ability to put the ball away. I continually put pressure on my opponent and use my athleticism and superb conditioning to intimidate my opponents.

STRATEGY AND GAME STYLE
- Net rusher. Primarily, objective will be to get to the net to try to end points.

TACTICS
- **Patterns of key importance:**
  Attack second serve by hitting approach and coming in.
  Attack short balls.
- **Serve-and-volley patterns:**
  Serve out wide on both sides and then volley to the open court.
  Stay back on second serve and then come to net off of return.
- **Serve:**
  Vary serve location and speed to get weak returns for easy volleys.

(continued next page)

(continued from previous page)

TECHNICAL DEVELOPMENT
- **Serve:**
  Needs more power and improved accuracy.
- **Volleys:**
  Needs to put away high balls at the net.
  Needs to hit deeper and firmer on balls lower than the net.

PSYCHOLOGICAL DEVELOPMENT
- No substantial improvement needed.

PHYSICAL DEVELOPMENT
- Take conditioning to the next level to keep intensity level up during three-set matches.

SCHEDULING AND PERIODIZATION
- Play at least one tournament a month.

GOAL SETTING
- **Performance goals:** (These are goals that you have a great deal of control over. A more detailed explanation is in chapter 7).
  Take seven lessons over the next month to improve technique on the serve and the volley.
  Serve: To improve power and location, hit 50 practice serves with targets three times a week.
  Volley: Volley-lob drill for 15 minutes three times a week.
  Conditioning: Volley-lob drill for 15 minutes three times a week.
- **Outcome goals:** (These are result goals that a player does not have control over.)
  Rating: Get a 4.5 NTRP rating by the end of the year.
  Tournaments: Win club singles.
  Individual: Beat that arrogant Arthur Jones!

DEVELOPMENTAL PLAN II
For the Aspiring World-Class Player

PLAYER: "Jane Smith"
PLAYER DESCRIPTION: Female, 13 years old, 5'6"
Ranked in the top 50 of USTA National rankings.
DEVELOPMENTAL TEAM LEADER: Coach's Name (USPTA or PTR Certified)

PLAYER EVALUATION
- Big, strong, aggressive baseline player.
- Hits hard off of both sides. Backhand is more solid, but hits more winners off the forehand.
- Likes to attack early in the points, often on the first shot.
- Tendency to be impatient and rush the point.
- Tactically, plays some patterns well. However, has not mastered the patterns that play into her strengths.
- Overall movement is adequate but could improve significantly. Moves well side to side. Needs improvement moving forward.
- Reasonable technique on the volley but is uncomfortable finishing off points at net.
- Forehand: Hits a lot of winners, good power.
- Power: Has natural power, good size, and excellent racket head speed.
- Serve is a potential weapon: Good arm action and power. Technique needs work.

LONG-TERM VISION
Plays an aggressive all-court game in which she has excellent first-strike capability. Takes command of the points early in the rally through a big serve, aggressive returns, and taking the ball early off the bounce on the ground strokes. Tactically plays aggressive, high-percentage tennis. Physically is in great condition and moves well in all aspects of the game. She uses her size and strength to physically dominate opponents. Psychologically, she projects a powerful, positive presence (PPP) on the court during her matches and is a fierce competitor who loves competition.

(continued next page)

(continued from previous page)

STRATEGY AND GAME STYLE
- Aggressive baseline player and finishes off numerous points at the net.
- Big serve to win free points either by ace or winner and/or attempts to elicit a weak response so as to take control of the point.
- Return games are aggressive, particularly on second serves.
- Backcourt play: Stays close to the baseline and takes the balls early. Plays aggressive powerful shot with high percentage.

TACTICS
- **Serve:** Develops serve patterns that play the opponent out wide on both sides, then hits to the open court with power. Plays power serve down the tee on both sides, looking for an ace or a reply that lands toward the middle of the court where she can take advantage.
- **Returns:** Plays aggressive, high-percentage returns crosscourt, highlighting power. Also hits the powerful neutralizing ball down the middle of the court. On second serves, often plays aggressive return down the line. If she hits a high-quality return and opponent is slow responding she comes to the net behind the shot.
- **Backcourt:** Takes command of the center of the court. When the ball lands in that area she is aggressive and attempts to take control off of that shot. Frequently takes the ball down the line (off of a crosscourt shot) with power when she has time to set up. A premium is put on pace and depth on her shots to keep her opponent at bay and enable her to control the points. When she hits a quality ground stroke in which her opponent is slow responding, she looks to move forward and finish off the point at net.

TECHNICAL DEVELOPMENT
- **Serve:** Needs to improve arm action and get more explosion up into the serve with her legs.
- **Ground strokes:** Needs to work on keeping good upper-body posture on low balls.
- **Volley:** Needs to shorten up swing and use more legs.

PSYCHOLOGICAL DEVELOPMENT
- Must continue to focus on playing one point at a time and executing to the best of her ability.
- Use positive self-talk at all times.

PHYSICAL DEVELOPMENT
- Develop a solid aerobic base as a foundation for her physical development.
- Develop strength in the quads and gluteus maximus for stability.

(continued next page)

(continued from previous page)

SCHEDULING AND PERIODIZATION
- Will compete in approximately 15 tournaments this year.
- Three tournaments in a row is maximum, followed by a minimum of two weeks of practice and rest.
- Will take October and November off from tournament play to work on development of her game and physical strength.

GOAL SETTING
- **Performance goals:**
  Long term (1 year): To perfect the down-the-line return patterns off of the second serve and develop the ability to finish off the point at net when appropriate.
  Medium (6 months): To be able to hit the return down the line with confidence and use it in a match at least five to six times and to follow it into the net once or twice.
  Short term (1 month): Will have partner hit me serves and I will work on the returns down the line for 15 minutes at least three times a week.
- **Outcome goals:**
  Long term (1 year): Achieve a WTA world ranking.
  Medium (6 months): Will play in the qualifying in four $10,000 events.
  Short term (4 weeks): Will enter $10,000 futures event and will ask for wild card into qualifying.

Embrace Your Playing Personality

> Your on-court instincts should be the driving force in developing a playing style and formulating match strategy.

Your personality is the key to developing the right game style and strategy for you. In Shakespeare's famous play *Hamlet*, Polonius advised, "To thine own self be true." That's good advice for tennis players, too.

Chris Evert

International Tennis Hall of Fame inductee and winner of 18 Grand Slam singles titles

Letting your on-court personality be the driving force behind the style of game you play is so important. Over the course of my playing career, I practiced hitting my volleys quite a bit. Although it wasn't my strength, I was a competent volleyer. But when it came time to play a match, being up at the net was not where I was comfortable. Even if I was hitting well, I knew that my best chance to win was on the baseline. Of course, I would come to the net to finish off points when necessary. However, if I could help it, I would stay at the baseline. That was the type of game style that was best for me. In order for you to play your best, you've got to follow your own natural instincts. If you compromise by playing in a style that doesn't suit you, you won't maximize your potential.

Your on-court instincts must be a determining factor in developing your playing style and formulating a match strategy. Being confident in what you're doing on the court is a huge key to success. You've got to believe in your game, otherwise you'll just be a ghost of yourself on the court. This chapter goes a long way in helping you discover what is your true on court personality. Nick thoroughly and accurately breaks down the different playing styles and how to determine which one you belong to. (And better still, how to beat all the others!)

I was basically a counterpuncher. That was my strategy. I waited for my opponent to give me an opportunity and then I took it. And coincidentally, that's me off the court as well. I'm not an overly aggressive person, rarely doing anything off the cuff. But the two don't always go hand-in-hand. A lot of serve-and-volleyers are actually passive people. There was never a more unassuming and laid back player off the court than Stefan Edberg. But on the court his instincts were to get to net and end the point as quickly and as aggressively as possible. So don't assume that because you behave a certain way off the court, you're suppose to play that way when you're on it. One of the great things about tennis is even though approaches can be similar, every unique personality manifests into its very own distinctive style.

When you combine two players with contrasting on court personalities, you have a recipe for a classic match. As in the cases of Borg-McEnroe, Lendl-Becker, and Martina and myself, the on-court instinct of one player was completely opposite of their opponent. I knew when I played Martina that she was going to pressure me all day long. It was my job to react to her aggression. I would make slight adjustments to my game, as would she, depending on the surface or the occasion. If we played on clay, Martina would be more selective about when she attacked net. If we met on grass, I knew I would have to take advantage every opportunity I got to be aggressive. But no matter what the surface, we always stayed within our basic personality traits and game style. I wasn't going to become a net rusher anymore than she was going to take part in thirty stroke baseline rallies. If I was going to beat her, I knew it had to be within the framework of playing smart, percentage, base-line tennis.

Having a solid understanding and familiarity with your own instincts and style will help determine how successful you will be. Being true to yourself and your game is the only way to go.

True Style and Strategy

If your style of play is not consistent with your personality, it will destroy your enjoyment, love, and passion for the game. Going to the courts day after day trying to play a game that disagrees with you will rub against the grain of who you are and how you express yourself. The results will be a disaster. It doesn't matter whether you are a weekend warrior, an aspiring junior, or a world-class player. If you want to be the best player you can be, your own unique personality must be the driving force behind the style of game you play and strategy you develop.

In the heat of a match, when the pressure is really on, great players go to the core of their game. You can feel and see their true personality coming through on the court in how they compete and try to win points. Their natural instincts take over to attack the net or dig in at the baseline when crunch time comes. They do what comes most naturally, what feels most comfortable, and what they have the most confidence in to succeed.

Think about it. Can you picture Andre Agassi or the Williams sisters, when the match is on the line, standing way behind the baseline and hitting conservative, high-percentage ground strokes and taking no risks? Of course not. They'd step into the court and pound ground strokes to take control of the point. Would an aggressive player like Pete Sampras stay back and trade ground strokes when it's crunch time? No. He would attack the net to put the ball away. These athletes play that way because that is who they are. Sure, such players can play tactics that are different from their fundamental style for a time, and they often do just that to gain an advantage in a match. But they could never do it as their primary strategy. If they did, they simply would not be the great players they are today.

The same holds true for you. If you are playing a strategy that is not true to your personality, you'll not only feel frustrated and miserable on the court but you also will wilt under the pressure of competition. This does not mean that you should be one-dimensional as a player. You should be able to adjust your play tactically when necessary and employ whatever strategy will work in a match. However, your overall game style and strategy should remain true to the person you are.

Apples and Oranges

When you listen to sports commentators on TV, many times they use the words "strategy" and "tactics" interchangeably, and the meanings of these words get convoluted. Even in books about tennis, it is often confusing and difficult to delineate between strategy and tactics. Yet, there is a profound difference.

Before I discuss different styles of play and how to choose what style you should play, let's clarify exactly what I mean by *style, strategy,* and *tactics.* Knowing the meaning of these terms will give you a deeper understanding of your current game, the game you want to develop, and your opponents' game and how to counter their style. A detailed discussion of tactics will be covered in chapter 3, but for now some general definitions will suffice.

Game Style

Game style means exactly what it implies: the style of game you like to play. (I'll get into detail on the four basic styles of player later in this chapter.) Your game style usually remains constant once you develop your skills. However, your style of play may evolve as your game matures. Pete Sampras, for example, was a ground-stroking, two-handed baseliner as a young junior. Yet, as he grew, he developed a one-handed backhand and an aggressive, net-rushing style of play. In contrast, Lindsay Davenport has played virtually the same style she started as a youngster throughout her entire career.

> She was one of the four highly-ranked 14-and-under players (two boys and two girls) whom I took to the top 14-and-under event in the world, called the Les Petits in France. I vividly remember the first time she played. This tall girl (5 feet 10 inches at 12 years of age) took huge swings at the ball and hit hard, flat ground strokes; and I remember thinking, *I can't believe she can keep the ball in the court. What incredible eye–hand coordination and power.* She was impressive throughout the tournament, reaching the finals before losing to a German player. But she left an impression that week that she had something special. Today, Lindsay Davenport—former number-one player in the world and a gold medalist—plays a very similar style to the one she played when she was 12 years old.

Your strategy is usually tied to your game style, to the extent that the two terms are often considered almost synonymous. Your game style almost always will determine your basic strategy.

Lindsay Davenport (second from left) played a similar style at 12 years old to the one she does today.

Strategy

Your strategy is your overall game plan that you employ during competition under almost all conditions and on most surfaces. Take Venus Williams: Her strategy is to serve big, be aggressive and powerful off the ground, and take control of the point early in the rally. She will play this basic strategy virtually every time she walks out on the court.

Tactics

Tactics are the specific shots and combinations of shots and maneuvers you use to win points on the court. One example is serving wide and coming in for the volley. Another tactic is hitting to the backhand of your opponent to elicit a defensive return. You make tactical adjustments to establish an advantage over your opponent, to neutralize or counter his strategy, or to adjust to environmental conditions.

The specific tactical adjustments you make during a match usually fall within the context of your overall strategy. Let's use Venus Williams again as an example. Venus might make a tactical adjustment during a match to come to the net a little more than usual or to hit to her opponent's forehand because that is her weaker side. But she would execute these adjustments without varying from her general strategy of hitting big and overpowering her opponent. In other words, she is not about to attack the net on every point, nor will she try to outlast her opponent from the backcourt. Just as a leopard doesn't change its spots, you should not make radical tactical changes that are contrary to your basic strategy.

I Gotta Be Me!

Be true to yourself, and develop a style of play consistent with your personality. That sounds like an obvious point, but it really is not. It is easy for players even at the professional level to lose their way when it comes to playing the right strategy. Sometimes you have to learn this lesson the hard way.

> Growing up on the fast, hard courts of northern California, I developed into an attacking net rusher who served and volleyed and came in to the net at every opportunity. This strategy fit my personality perfectly. I was impatient and loved to be aggressive. Unfortunately, because there were no clay courts in my area, I had little clay-court experience. So, when I became a professional player and competed all over the world, I was undaunted by my inexperience on clay. I simply went out and played as I would on hard courts, serving and volleying and attacking the net. I became pretty good at moving on the slow clay and finding the best ways to attack the net. Remarkably, I was able to beat some highly ranked players on clay. I even reached the quarterfinals and semifinals of some big clay-court events. Those results helped me break the top 50 in the world for the first time.
>
> Shortly afterward, a veteran coach who was out on the tour suggested that I change my overall style and strategy to become not only a better clay-court player but also a better all-around player. He said all I needed to do was have a more balanced attack, stay back and work the points, and temper my

attacking style. I was only 22 at the time, still looking to get better, and very suggestible. So I bought into his advice hook, line, and sinker.

I practiced my ground strokes religiously and improved my consistency so that I was more comfortable off the ground. I stayed back more in my practice matches and worked the points. Armed with my new style and strategy, I went back out on tour to compete. What a disaster! I lost 10 first-round matches in a row. Not only did my ranking and confidence drop, but worst of all, I hated the way I was playing. It was no fun.

What went wrong? First of all, it was a poorly-devised developmental plan. But the core issue was that my new style of play was totally inconsistent with my personality. It also minimized my best weapons (my volleys and quickness at the net) that were the foundation of my confidence. The result was that I hit my ground strokes better, but everything else fell apart. What I should have done was stick with my basic style and strategy, adjusting my tactics when I played on clay and simply refining and improving the other aspects of my game.

I paid a dear price for learning this simple, but profound, lesson. Don't make the same mistake. Remember, if anyone tries to get you to play a strategy that is not consistent with your personality, simply tell him, "I've got to be me," and stick with your game.

Five Keys to Establishing a Successful Strategy

Following are five keys to help you establish the style that is right for you—personality, physical traits, weapons, weaknesses, and patterns of play. As you read about these five keys, you will see that they are all inextricably tied together. If you can incorporate these five areas into your style, then you will not only take a big step toward becoming the best player you can be but you will have a blast playing the game.

Personality

I have already explained at length why this is so important. However, you need to evaluate some specific things about your personality. Are you extremely patient and passive on the court, and do you tend to be averse to risk taking? If you have these types of characteristics, they are clear indications that you should adopt a fairly conservative style, such as counterpuncher or baseline player. Conversely, if you are impatient, over-eager for immediate rewards, and don't like to concentrate for long periods, than these types of personality traits should lead you toward a more aggressive style, such as aggressive baseliner or net rusher.

A Note to Parents and Coaches

Most of the time, young players' game style and strategy will evolve naturally, provided they are not forced into a particular way of playing. However, sometimes players lock themselves into playing a particular style because they win at an early stage. This may not be the best style in the long term. Another factor is that they might be extremely small at a young age, then grow into a big athlete as they mature. Because of these factors, I recommend three things to keep in mind:

1. Young players, ages 8 to 14, should learn a good technical and tactical foundation for all aspects of the game so that they are not limited later on if their style of game or strategy changes.

2. It is important to know and understand the basic growth and developmental stages of children, from early childhood to after puberty. This way you can assess what a child's physical abilities should be at a certain age and how much the child may develop as she physically matures.

3. If the player is serious about improving, help him establish a vision of the ultimate player he wants to be and keep it consistent with his personality.

Physical Traits

The physical traits you possess also should be incorporated into and maximized by the style you develop. If you are an adult, you probably already know exactly what those skills are. This is not as easy to determine for young, aspiring players. Their physical attributes may change as they mature. This underscores the importance of learning all the basic skills early on so that they are not limited in the future. Some of the physical factors to consider include height, weight, speed, agility, coordination, and muscular strength.

Physical characteristics do affect what strategy you employ. Let's say you are tall but not very quick. You might want to consider developing a "first-strike" type of style, in which you try to take control of the point early in the rally either with your serve, your return of serve, or your first shot. Your height will probably enable you to hit with power. If you can take control of the point early, your opponent won't be able to run you back and forth on the court, which will minimize your lack of speed and quickness. On the other hand, if you are short and a good mover but don't possess a lot of power, you might develop consistent ground strokes and passing shots. Also, work to enhance your defensive skills. This way you can highlight your movement, play consistently, and effectively counter bigger, more powerful players.

Weapons

Most players naturally develop weapons starting from a young age. First, know what your strengths are. Many players fool themselves, believing they have a better volley or a more powerful forehand than they actually have. Consult with your developmental team leader (DTL) to help you identify your strengths; your objective should be to integrate those weapons with your style of play. Your style should maximize the use of those weapons, such as running around the backhand to hit your powerful forehand as often as possible or developing consistency off the ground to take advantage of your speed.

Weaknesses

Just as you should maximize your strengths, you should minimize your weaknesses. The correct style makes it difficult for your opponent to exploit your weaknesses. For example, Lindsay Davenport is not one of the best movers on the women's tour (although I can't really call it a weakness). In most of her matches, however, her movement is not a factor because her basic strategy is to take control of the point with power right from the first ball. By dictating the pace to her opponent, Lindsay makes it difficult to get her on the run.

Patterns of Play

The right style for your game should set up specific patterns of play that make it easier for you to win the point. This is tied in to the last two keys of maximizing your strengths and minimizing your weaknesses. You want to force your opponent to play to your weapons and prevent her from finding your weakness on the court. For example, if you have a big forehand and a weak backhand, look to run around your backhand and hit an inside-out forehand. That lets you hit your best shot, positions you on the court to make it more difficult for your opponent to find your backhand, and forces your opponent to hit back to your strength.

Basic Game Styles and Strategies

There are four game styles that constitute the primary strategies for all players. Learning about these styles accomplishes three important things. First, of course, is to understand what those styles are. Second, it will enable you to determine the best style for you or confirm that you are in fact playing the right style. And third, it will help you to recognize the different styles your opponents will play so that you can understand how to counter them.

For each style of play, I will give a brief description of the typical play and skill patterns demanded by that style of play. I will also list the keys to

A few years ago at the U.S. Open, Brad Gilbert and I went out to the back courts to watch a junior match involving one of the top U.S. juniors. He was playing against a young Australian. Brad wanted to see what kind of prospect the American was. He was big and strong, possessed a powerful serve, and played an aggressive ground-stroke game. However, after the first few games, Brad and I started to notice what an outstanding counterpuncher the young Australian was. He was very fast, made few mistakes, and seemed to have an answer for everything the American hit at him. Brad turned to me and said, "Our guy is good, but I really like this Australian kid. He's a player! Smart, fast, good athlete, competes well, no big weapons, but he can develop those." I said, "I couldn't agree more. This kid has a great counterpunching style, and if he develops a little more power and becomes more of an all-court player, he will be one hell of a player." We walked away after the Australian won the first set and Brad reiterated, "That kid is going to be a player!" Well, we were both right, but neither one of us could have predicted that he would get so good so quickly. You see, three and a half years later, the young Australian Lleyton Hewitt won the 2001 U.S. Open men's singles and then the 2002 Wimbledon Championship, using a combination of superb counterpunching with subtle interjections of all-court play, to become the youngest number one–ranked player in the modern game.

Lleyton Hewitt showed signs of greatness even as a junior.

© Lance Jeffrey

success for each style. That way, you can determine what your current style is, evaluate if it is best for you, and identify the key components needed to successfully execute your personal game style.

The four primary game styles are counterpuncher, aggressive baseliner, all-court player, and net rusher. (I call this last style of play "net rusher" instead of "serve and volleyer," as it is often called, because the term "net rusher" more adequately describes a player who constantly attacks the net.) Although countless variations are possible within these four broad categories, almost all players fall into one of them. Because you should develop a style of play that is consistent with and that best utilizes your own personal characteristics, your style and strategy will be unique. In fact, no two players are exactly alike.

Counterpuncher

Counterpunchers are basically defensive baseline players who react to their opponents' shots. Players who use this style of play usually allow their opponents to dictate play, and then they counter. Counterpunchers will usually play farther back in the court than aggressive baseliners, often far behind the baseline, and usually hit ground strokes with a higher net clearance and more spin. Their emphasis is on depth, consistency, control, and retrieving every ball. Such players usually have accurate passing shots, a fine touch on lobs, and are effective at neutralizing their opponents' power and attacking play.

Counterpunchers are often denigrated by being called "pushers." But at the highest levels of play, it is an effective strategy for players with speed, endurance, clay-court proficiency, and a lack of a big weapon. However, this type of player is most often found in junior tennis or adult recreational tennis. Few world-class players today employ a true counterpuncher style as their primary strategy. The reason is that the pros consistently hit such powerful shots that if a player is always waiting to counter, he may be hit right off the court. All players at the professional level, however, can employ a counterpunching tactic if necessary in a match. Examples of successful counterpunchers in the professional game are Sanchez-Vicario and Conchita Martinez of Spain.

PERSONALITY

Counterpunchers must be mentally tough. Successful counterpunchers must have a "never-give-up" attitude, with a willingness to stay out on the court as long as necessary to win a point and to win the match. They must also have patience. Relying on consistency, counterpunchers will seldom force the issue during a rally unless presented with an easy put-away. Counterpunchers are also cautious and not usually risk takers. For counterpunchers, the reward of taking more than minimal risks is not as great as in playing it safe.

Arantxa Sanchez-Vicario epitomized the counterpunching style.

© Lance Jeffrey

PHYSICAL TRAITS

Counterpunchers have a high level of fitness and consistently win matches by outlasting opponents. Running down every last shot takes its toll, however, so counterpunchers need to have excellent aerobic endurance, as well as good anaerobic power for the speed to run down shots. Successful counterpunchers also have good movement. If you lack speed, have slow reactions, or have poor footwork when trying to cover the court, the counterpunching game is the wrong style for you.

SKILLS AND STRENGTHS

In order to successfully execute the counterpunching style you need to possess consistent ground strokes and good ball control, which are the cornerstones of the counterpunchers game. Counterpunchers should have excellent passing shots and good offensive and defensive lobs, and be good hitters on the run because it does no good to run a ball down and not be able to execute a good shot.

TACTICS

In order to be successful tactically counterpunchers must understand and execute high percentage shot selection. They will need good neutralizing patterns. For example, when an opponent hits an aggressive down-the-line shot, the counterpuncher responds with a deep, looping shot crosscourt, which is difficult to attack. They also need the ability to move the ball around and keep it away from your opponents weapons and exploit a players weakness. Finally, good defensive tactics can get counterpunchers out of trouble like the ability to hit a good defensive lob while on a dead run.

CRITICAL PATTERNS OF PLAY

These are patterns that good counterpunchers must possess:

- Basic high-percentage crosscourt rally
- Two-shot passing shots: first ball down crosscourt, second ball pass
- Crosscourt rally, then change direction down the line
- Open up the court with angles, then hit to the open court

Aggressive Baseliner

Aggressive baseliners also rely on their ground strokes, but they play close to or in front of the baseline and choose to dictate play with their aggressive, powerful shots. Typically, aggressive baseliners have at least one true weapon off the ground. Most often that shot is a big forehand, but many aggressive baseliners have the ability to hit winners even from their weaker side. Players who are successful at this style are often extremely quick and agile. They are usually effective on all surfaces, and are particularly adept on a slow-to-medium-paced court. Usually they possess good returns of serve and often use their own serves to set up their weapons off the ground.

Examples of this type of player in the professional ranks are easy to find, as some of today's best players have been aggressive baseliners. Andre Agassi, Venus and Serena Williams, and Lindsay Davenport are prime examples of this type of play.

PERSONALITY

Aggressive baseliners are not afraid to attempt to hit winners. This type of player is aggressive and would rather make it happen herself than wait patiently for an opportunity to attack.

As an aggressive baseliner, Andre Agassi is relentlessly aggressive off both sides.

© Lance Jeffrey

PHYSICAL TRAITS

Players with a wide range of physical skills and body types can become successful aggressive baseliners. Unlike counterpunchers, in whom the lack of physical attributes presents a real handicap, aggressive baseliners can be tall or short, slow or quick, thick or thin. Aggressive baseliners usually have excellent power on their ground strokes. This style does not necessarily require players to be quick and agile—though it helps. However, these players must have the ability to set up in proper position and in good balance to allow them to tee off on their shots.

SKILLS AND STRENGTHS

In order to successfully execute the aggressive baseline style this player needs to possess good, sound, aggressive return of serve and the ability to take the ball early in order to control the points. They also need good control and variety on the serve in order to help set up the point so that they can use their ground strokes to end the point.

TACTICS

Aggressive baseliners need to know how to set the points up tactically to hit their big weapons. This requires that they use their serves intelligently to set up the point to their weapons as well as establish aggressive return pattern, which helps them get in control of the point quickly.

CRITICAL PATTERNS OF PLAY

The following are patterns that an aggressive baseliner needs to possess.

- Serve out wide on either side to set up their strength
- Serve to the body on either side, then step around to hit their weapon
- Serve to the tee to step around and hit their weapon
- Inside-out, ground-stroke patterns
- Change of direction from crosscourt to down the line
- Open up the court by hitting angles then hit to the open court

All-Court Player

All-court players are capable of playing all styles of play. The particular strategy they employ during a match depends on the situation. They usually are athletic and fit. All-court players tend to vacillate between offensive shots and neutralizing play. They often (but not always) do not have a single clear-cut weapon, but they do have the ability to use nearly all parts of their game offensively to win matches. Keep in mind, however, that few players actually fit this technical description of an all-court player. Usually a player has a clear preference for being either at the baseline or at the net. Examples of all-court players include Todd Martin and Martina Hingis.

A couple of years ago, I was sitting in the indoor mall underneath the Grand Hyatt in Melbourne, Australia, eating dinner with a young American pro Justin Gimelstob who was playing in the Australian Open. After a few minutes, Martina Hingis—who was a friend of Justin's and seeded first in the women's tournament—sat down and joined us for some light conversation. The discussion quickly turned to her upcoming match and her draw. It was fascinating to hear her explain how she was planning to play each player if she in fact won. The confidence she had in every aspect of her game became apparent. "Well, against her, I will play steady and move her around," "Against this one, I have to come in to the net more," and so on. What stood out in my mind was that she truly exemplified what it means to be an all-court player. This was the perfect style for her bright and crafty tactical mind and one that complemented her excellent all-around, yet not overpowering, game. Martina went on to win the event that year, as she used her all-court game to perfection.

© Lance Jeffrey

All-court player Martina Hingis is extremely comfortable in the backcourt or at the net.

PERSONALITY

All-court players are problem solvers. They like to think their way through matches. They excel at analyzing their opponents and figuring out the tactics that works best. These players are not afraid to adjust and adapt in the middle of a match, often as many times as necessary to win. All-court players also tend to get bored playing one way. Like an artist, they enjoy using all their talents.

PHYSICAL TRAITS

No definitive characteristics apply to this type of player. However, the best all-court players are in top physical condition and are athletic enough to be able to adjust and adapt according to the demands of the competition.

SKILLS AND STRENGTHS

An all-court player needs to have a well-rounded game—good technique and skills in both the backcourt and at the net in order to be able to play effectively in all areas of the court. They need to possess good ball control in order to manipulate the points.

TACTICS

All-court players are aware of how a match is evolving tactically so that they are able to make adjustments. They have a good understanding of basic patterns of play from all areas of the court.

CRITICAL PATTERNS OF PLAY

All-court players really should be able to understand and execute at least a few basic patterns from each phase of the game.

- Basic serve-and-volley patterns
- Basic serve-and-stay-back patterns off of wide, tee, and body serves
- Basic approach patterns: down the line, inside out, and off of return
- Basic backcourt patterns: crosscourt rally, crosscourt change of direction, inside out, and opening up court with angles

Net Rusher

Net rushers put enormous pressure on their opponents, attacking the net behind an approach shot or behind their serves to put the ball away with a volley. The serve is often a weapon, or at least extremely effective, in keeping their opponents off balance. Net rushers usually possess outstanding volleys and an understanding of net coverage and positioning. They also tend to be good athletes, with the movement skills to get to the net quickly and the agility and explosiveness to cover the net, as well as to scramble back to cover the lob. Points typically are won quickly, as their objective is to put their opponents constantly under pressure by attacking the net.

Players who exemplify this type of game style include Greg Rusedski and Pete Sampras (who has recently evolved into more of a serve and volleyer than he was early in his career). There currently aren't very many net rushers on the women's tour—Jana Novotna and Martina Navratilova being the last and best to play this style.

PERSONALITY

Net rushers possess an aggressive on-court personality. They want to take control of the point as soon as they can and end the point with one shot. They are also risk takers. Rushing the net is inherently a high-risk strategy that rewards aggressive players and punishes the tentative. Net rushers have great intensity and concentration for short periods. They don't like to play long points and must beware of becoming impatient and coming in at the wrong time.

PHYSICAL TRAITS

Athleticism is critical to net rushers' success. The better their speed, agility, and overall athleticism, the more effective they will be in this style of play.

Net rusher Greg Rusedski attacks the net whenever possible.

© Lance Jeffrey

Excellent anaerobic power allows net rushers to sprint to the net, lunge for the ball, and recover quickly. Although it is not an absolute requirement, height gives net rushers an advantage on the serve. Long strides allow them to get to the net quickly, and a long reach allows them to cover the net more effectively.

SKILLS AND STRENGTHS

Net rushers need to possess excellent serve, control, variety, disguise, and power in order to serve and volley. They obviously need to have good eye-hand coordination, excellent technique and skill at the net and an effective transition game such as good slice approach. Being able to get back to cover the lob and put the ball away with a smash is essential.

TACTICS

Good net rushers have good awareness to recognize an opportunity to attack the net and when it is not smart to take the risk. They know what kind of shot is best to come in behind and how to hit it. A major tactic for net rushers is to chip and charge against the opponent's second serve. It may be the shortest ball they see on the court. A little known secret about good net rushers is that they almost always play high percentage volleys. They simply take what their opponent gives them, playing the high-percentage volley to set up the winner on the second shot.

CRITICAL PATTERNS OF PLAY

Here are a few patterns that are a must for the net rusher.

- Serve out wide on either side and know the options from three basic returns.
- Serve to the body on either side. Know your options.
- Serve to the tee on deuce and ad.
- Approach down the line.
- Approach from midcourt, inside out.
- Approach off the return, down the line.

Once you have determined or start to evolve into your primary style of play, the next step is to develop the strategy, patterns, tactics, and weapons necessary to implement that particular game style. Tailoring your practices and choosing appropriate drills specifically designed to improve a particular style of play are keys to maximizing your time on the court. This is where a coach can help design an effective practice routine. I will address this further in chapter 6.

Countering Your Opponent's Style

Your style of play should maximize your strengths and minimize your weaknesses. Your number one objective is to impose your basic strategy on your opponent. But you also should be able to recognize your opponent's style of play and make subtle tactical adjustments to expose the vulnerable aspects of your opponent's game. While your basic strategy may stay the same, the most effective tactics against one player may not be effective against another. It is therefore important that you have some general tactical guidelines when dealing with specific styles of play. I have outlined a few key tactical principles that can be used against the four different styles of play.

Countering Counterpunchers

1. Focus on finishing the point, and expect to hit extra shots to accomplish this goal.

2. Be patient. Play patterns and wait for an opportunity. Don't go for an outright winner prematurely.

3 Attack whenever a good opportunity presents itself.

4. When you are out of position, don't overhit, but hit a neutralizing shot, as your opponent is unlikely to take advantage of your vulnerable position.

5. Frequently hit behind your opponent to counter their speed.

Countering Aggressive Baseliners

1. Attempt to dictate the point right from the start of the point, as opposed to reacting to your opponent. Focus on making a quality first shot.

2. Occasionally hit out wide to your opponent's strength to catch him off guard then play back to their weakness.

3. Vary the speed and location of your serve to keep your opponent out of rhythm. For example, serve into your opponent's body more frequently.

4. Keep the ball out of your opponent's "power zone." Vary the pace of your shots and use a slice if appropriate.

Countering All-Court Players

1. Because all-court players usually don't have a dominant weapon, take advantage of this opportunity to play with patterns that play into your strength.

2. Be prepared for your opponent to change tactics more than once if she is losing the match. Make tactical adjustments that clearly stay within your basic strategy.

3. Attempt to control the point from the start, which limits your opponent's ability to play their game.

Countering Net Rushers

1. Attempt to get as many first serves back in play as possible.

2. Put your returns down at your opponent's feet.

3. Use an offensive lob, particularly early in the match, to keep your opponent off the net.

4. Focus on making two-shot passes. Get the ball down low on the first pass, and then hit it by your opponent on the second.

5. Focus on making the passing shot and avoid the tendency to be rushed into making an error.

6. Consider coming into the net more frequently than usual to take the net from your opponent.

7. Attack and exploit your opponent's second serve.

A lot of information is presented in this chapter, but don't let that distract you from the fundamental issue. Develop a style and strategy consistent with your personality. Within this context, you can increase your understanding of what you need to do to maximize your game. If you do this it will be a huge step in becoming the best player you can be. This also relates to tactics, which I will discuss in the next chapter.

CHAPTER 3

Customize Tactics

> "In the heat of the battle, stay on track by focusing on shots and tactical adjustments that reinforce your overall match strategy."

Tactics are the adjustments, maneuvers, specific shots, and combinations of shots that you use during the course of a point or a match. These adjustments are done to give you the edge over your opponent, to neutralize or counter his strategy, or to adjust to environmental conditions. However, there are many things to consider as you approach tactics.

There are general tactics that apply to all players, such as hitting a crosscourt shot over the low part of the net or serving to your opponent's weakness. I call these "generic tactics," which basically apply to all players. But everyone has a uniquely different game style and strategy, and so the right tactics for one player may not necessarily be the right tactics for you. Therefore the particular adjustments you should make on the court that highlight your strengths and minimize your weaknesses are what I call your "personal tactics." For example, a common tactical move on important points is to get a high percentage of first serves in. However, would you tell Pete Sampras not to go for an ace down the middle of the court on a breaking point, or tell Venus Williams not to hit swinging forehand volleys from midcourt because they are low-percentage shots? Of course you wouldn't.

Nick Bollettieri

Coach of 7 No. I world-ranked players, including Andre Agassi and Monica Seles

You can have the greatest technique in the world but if you don't understand tactics and shot selection you won't be in the winners circle very often. This is true in any sport. Tiger Woods has tremendous technical skills, but so do many of the other top golfers. What makes him stand out from the rest is that he understands his own game so well he knows exactly what shot he is capable of at every moment and makes the right choice when the tournament is on the line. Andre Agassi is the same way. He is one of the greatest ball strikers who has ever played, but most people don't realize that his tactical skills are just as good as his strokes! He plays the aggressive ground-stroking style to perfection, choosing high percentage, offensive shots until he gets a ball he can attack. That is why I believe this chapter is so important. It will help you concentrate on making the correct tactical moves that will favor you at crucial times. So take the time to read this chapter carefully, apply its principles and I guarantee you it will be time well spent.

Consider these two general guidelines as you think about tactics:

• Rule 1. You should make your tactical adjustments within the context of your own personal strategy. In other words, you should always be looking to highlight your strengths and minimize your weaknesses.

• Rule 2. Avoid your opponent's strengths and attack her weaknesses. If you have any questions about rule 2 during a match, refer to rule 1.

Generic Tactics

Players need to know and execute percentage plays, patterns, and basic tactics regardless of their individual game styles. These are the foundations of good tennis. Understanding and mastering these generic tactics allow you to take full advantage of your own individual style of play.

Percentage Tennis

The general goal in high-percentage tennis is to make fewer errors while forcing your opponent into making more errors. You can accomplish this through sound shot selection and high-percentage patterns that maximize your strengths and minimize your weaknesses.

In the fall of 1983, I was 27 and had been playing on the tour for seven years. In the first round of a tour event in Nancy, France, I was scheduled to play the top junior in the world. The previous week, he had won the German satellite segment (a series of entry-level professional tournaments that young players use to earn their way into the major pro tour). The guys in the locker room gave me the rundown on this youngster who was creating quite a stir in the tennis world. "Super talent," they said. "What does he play like?" I asked. They told me he had an excellent backhand, a very good serve, and a great net game. He attacks the net relentlessly. Well, I was a veteran of the tour, and I knew how I was going to play. I was going to serve and volley and attack the net.

When we went out to play our match, my opponent won the toss and elected to serve. On the first point, he served and came into the net behind it. I blocked the return, he volleyed to the open court, and I ran it down and hit a winner. On the second point, he served and volleyed, and I hit another winner. Two more points yielded the same results. I had played an unbelievable first game and broke him at love.

We changed sides, and I acted as if this was just a routine game for me. From that point on, my opponent stopped serving and volleying for the rest of the match. I had intimidated him into staying back and going against his basic strategy. This was exactly what I wanted to do because it gave me the opportunity to attack the net at will. The result was a blowout. I beat him 6–1, 6–2.

After the match I wanted to tell my opponent that he should have stuck with his game style, but I didn't know him, and somehow I knew he probably would not make that mistake again. He did not. My opponent that day was Stefan Edberg, the great Swedish star, who ascended to the number-one ranking in the world and won seven Grand Slam singles titles. I saw Edberg make that same mistake—losing sight of his strategy and stop attacking the net—only one other time. And I believe it cost him the match. It was against Michael Chang in the final of the 1989 French Open. It turned out to be one of the biggest matches of his life. If he had won Roland Garros that day, he would have finished his career having won all four Grand Slam titles. That would have made him only the fifth man in history to achieve that feat. The moral of the story, of course, is that it usually does not pay to deviate from your basic strategy.

Percentage tennis is a relative term. A safe and reliable tactic or shot for one player may be a difficult or risky play for another. High-percentage shot selection, therefore, will vary according to each player's skills. The key to playing percentage tennis is to make sure you know your own game, know what your strengths and weaknesses are, and know how to set up points to play your best shots and patterns. Some basic principles of high-percentage tennis, however, are generally applicable to all players.

THE FOUR HORSEMEN

You may not realize it, but during every point you play, you make a split-second decision to hit one of four different types of shots: offensive, building, neutral, or defensive. The shot you select in that split second goes a long way toward determining whether you play a good tactical point.

Distinguishing among the four different kinds of shots is not always easy. Sometimes it is determined by the position you are in on the court. Sometimes it is determined by your skill level or particular style of play. As a general guide, here's a brief explanation of the different shots and a guide for when to hit each one.

* **Offensive**—The intent of an offensive shot is either to win the point outright or to hurt your opponent, putting him on the defensive and enabling you to win the point on the next shot. The time to hit an offensive shot is when the ball is right where you like it, at a good height and comfortable pace, and when you are in excellent court position and in good balance to execute your shot.

Offensive shot—Young German star Tommy Haas prepares to rip a forehand from inside the baseline.

© Lance Jeffrey

• **Building**—A building, or setup, shot is intended to put you in position to take control of the point or to win the point on the next couple of shots. Often, this is the first shot in a particular pattern or combination of shots. The height of the ball may not be quite in your sweet spot, certainly not enough to tee off on the ball. However, when the placement and pace of your opponent's shot have not put you in a precarious position and you are in position and in balance to execute your stroke properly, you should consider hitting a building shot. An example is when your opponent hits a shot that lands beyond the service line but not deep enough to move you back or wide enough to make you run.

Building shot—Jennifer Capriati hits an aggressive forehand to build the point.

© Lance Jeffrey

Neutral shot—Todd Martin hits a neutralizing backhand slice.

© Lance Jeffrey

- **Neutral**—Use a neutral shot when you are responding to an opponent's quality shot. You may hit the ball with good pace, depth, or placement; and though it doesn't put you in a very precarious position, it is too difficult to try to hit a forcing shot of your own. Your intention is to counter your opponent's shot with one that will neutralize your opponent's momentary advantage. Say your opponent hits a deep, hard shot to your backhand. A neutralizing shot would be to hit a looping, deep topspin ground stroke, which gives you time to recover, or a slice backhand, which will keep the ball low and out of your opponent's strike zone.

- **Defensive**—Use a defensive shot when you are in desperate trouble. Your opponent has hit a shot with extremely good pace, depth, or placement (or all of these combined) and you are struggling just to reach the ball or deal with her shot. Your intent here is to find a way to stay in the point. An example of a defensive shot is to hit a high lob while on a dead run.

Defensive shot—Gustavo Kuerten hits a defensive shot to try and stay in the point.

© Lance Jeffrey

HIGH-PERCENTAGE PRINCIPLES

Regardless of your style of play or game strategy, you need to understand several generic principles to play high-percentage tennis. On every shot, you must take into consideration the match situation at the time.

1. Know your game and your strengths and weaknesses.
2. Recognize offensive, neutral, and defensive positions.
3. Keep the ball in play.
4. Adjust to the playing conditions.
5. Hit to large target areas on the court.
6. Get good net clearance on your ground strokes.
7. Impart spin to the ball to enhance control.
8. Temper the speed of your shot for more control when trying to hit to a precise location. *More speed equals less control.*
9. Hit to larger target areas when you hit with power.
10. Hit crosscourt, which gives you the longest range to hit the ball into the court from corner to corner and the lowest part of the net to hit over (three feet in the center of the net).

PLAYING THE ZONES

How many times have you seen players make these mistakes during matches? A ball lands close to the net, and the player runs forward to get to the ball, only to hit it into the middle of the net or drive it 10 feet past the baseline. Or a ball lands two feet past the service line, smack in the middle of the court, and the player does not use the opportunity to take the offensive. How about seeing a player try to hit a winner off a ball that lands inches from the baseline.

It's as if these players were oblivious to where and how the ball landed on their side of the court. The shots they chose to hit were inappropriate considering their position on the court or were too risky or difficult for the situation, and they lost the opportunity to take control of the point.

These mistakes are not limited to club players. Quite the contrary. Many of the top young pros are guilty of the same poor decisions. To help you make better decisions in shot selection and better recognize when opportunities present themselves—and don't present themselves—I have broken down the court into various zones (see figure 3.1).

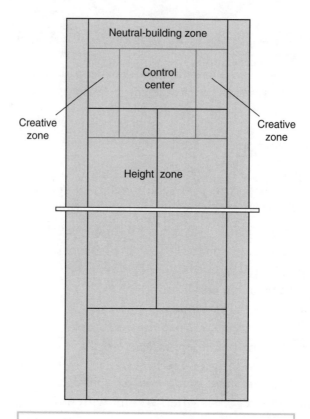

Figure 3.1   Court zones.

- **Neutral-building zone**—This is the area that is within four to five feet of the baseline. You are not going to hit many winners from this position. You should either try to neutralize your opponent or hit a building shot to elicit a weak reply to get into a better position (see figure 3.2).

- **Height zone**—This area starts from a few feet inside the service line and extends right up to the net. The number-one factor here is the height of the ball when you reach it. If the ball is above the level of the net, you are in an offensive position. If the ball is at or just slightly below the level of the net, you should hit a building shot, with the intent of setting up an opportunity to win the point on the next shot. If the ball is well below the level of the net, you are in a neutralizing position. Finally, if you are struggling just to get to the ball, you are in a defensive position (see figure 3.3).

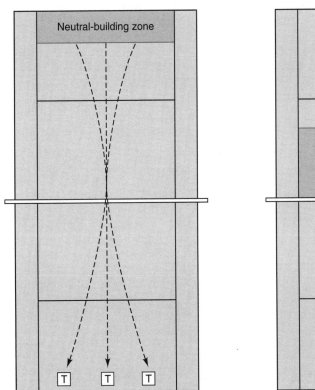

Figure 3.2 Neutral-building zone.

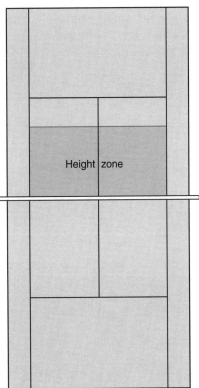

Figure 3.3 Height zone.

The next time you get a short ball on the court, recognize that what is most important is the height of the ball when you get to it. Use that as your guideline in choosing what kind of shot to hit, and you'll find you will rarely choose the wrong shot.

• **Control center**—This is the area right in the middle of the court (see figure 3.4). Up and back, it begins just inside the service line and extends back to about five or six feet from the baseline. From side to side, it extends about five feet in either direction from the center service line. When your opponent hits a ball into this area, you should look to take control of the point if not win it outright. Obviously, what you do depends on the height and pace of your opponent's shot, but a ball that lands in this area is generally an opportunity to put yourself in the driver's seat.

• **Creative zones**—The creative zones are the sections of the court to the left and right of the control center (see figure 3.5). When you get a low-quality shot in this area, you have the opportunity to be creative. By creative I mean you have three primary options: you can hit down the line, deep crosscourt, or at a sharp angle to open up the court. Any one of these shots can hurt your opponent and put you in a position to end the point on the next shot.

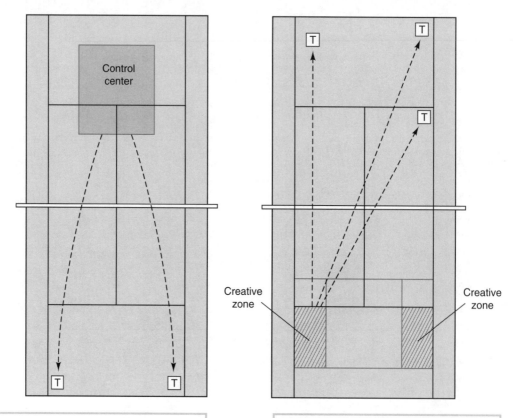

Figure 3.4 Control center.

Figure 3.5 Creative zones.

Now I don't want you to go out and divide the court into all these different zones. It would get much too complicated. However, I would advise you to focus on only one of these zones at a time. Let's take the control center as an example. When you go out to practice, be aware of when the ball lands in that area. Better yet, if you have rubber targets that lie flat on the court, you can outline the area and see whether it is a good opportunity to take control of the point. You will be amazed at how many more opportunities you will have to attack and how much better your shot selection will be. Conversely, make a concerted effort to keep your own shots out of your opponent's control center.

Patterns of Play

Regardless of your level of tennis, you should play many of the same patterns that the world-class professionals use. The basic difference between the pros and local players at the club, top juniors, and collegiate players is that the professionals understand which patterns to use at which times, the quality of their shots is better, and they execute those patterns extremely well.

You may only play two or three patterns with a high degree of confidence. Many pros don't play more than three or four basic patterns most of the time. I'd like you to understand three things from this section. First, I want to give you at least a basic understanding of the key patterns of play for the five major areas of the game: serving, returning, backcourt play, transition (or approaching the net), and serve and volley. Second, I want to enhance your understanding of how to execute these patterns well. Finally, I want to help you add some of these key patterns to your repertoire. Mastering these patterns of play will help you execute your strategy more effectively. Some keys to success include the following:

- **Maximize your strengths.** Yes, I know you have heard me say this before, but it is so important. Use your strengths! If your forehand is your big weapon, set up patterns that play into your forehand.

- **Minimize your weaknesses.** If your backhand is your weakness, don't use patterns that will force you to hit a lot of backhands. You should also use counterpatterns.

- **Use counterpatterns.** A counterpattern (also called a pattern breaker) is when you change an existing pattern that is being played to avoid playing your weakness or to avoid your opponent's strength. For example, your opponent is playing his powerful forehand to your weak forehand. Your counterpattern is to hit your forehand down the line to force him into a crosscourt rally involving your backhand.

A few years ago I was on the practice court with Jan-Michael Gambill, and he was practicing with Andre Agassi in preparation for a Davis Cup match against Belgium. Andre was doing a great job of serving the kick serve out wide on the add court, pulling Jan-Michael off the court, then hitting the next shot to the open court. On the kick serve, Andre would toss the ball over his head to get the desired spin. This gave away that he was going to hit that type of serve out wide. So I asked him whether he was ever concerned about getting more disguise on the serve. He said, "It is great if you can get the disguise and the execution. But the bottom line is, if I get a good kick that pulls him out wide and then hit to the open court and he is not able to counter that pattern, then I am not so worried about the disguise factor. I have found that, if you execute the pattern well, most of the time it doesn't matter whether or not the guy knows it's coming."

Andre Agassi, Jan-Michael Gambill, and Nick Saviano after a workout.

• **Use a quality first shot.** Hitting a quality first shot to start a pattern forces your opponent to play into your hands or possibly to try a low-percentage, risky shot. When she does, then you can respond to her shot with a high-percentage shot. In most cases this automatically puts your opponent on the defensive—and might possibly even win the point outright.

• **Winning the point is not the only goal.** Often the idea behind using a certain pattern is to create doubt or confusion in your opponent.

For example, even though your game style is to stay back, you might use a serve-and-volley pattern on a point to keep your opponent off balance. The more your opponent is uncomfortable or has to guess on the court, the more effective your game.

• **Mastery of a few patterns is better than mediocrity of many.** It may seem obvious, but it's better to have a high level of skill with few patterns than to have a low level of skill with many different patterns. So, keep in mind that you don't have to learn all of the following patterns of play. No player is a master of all.

Below are listed the four game styles and the types of patterns for each that you need to have in your repertoire to be successful. For example, everyone should have good serve-and-return patterns, whereas counterpunchers do not need to be skilled in the patterns of serve and volley. Therefore, serve and volley is not listed for counterpunchers.

1. Counterpuncher—Serve, return, backcourt
2. Aggressive baseliner—Serve, return, backcourt, transition
3. All-court player—Serve, return, backcourt, transition, serve and volley
4. Net rusher—Serve, return, serve and volley, transition

In the following sections I have described and explained the most common and important patterns in each area of the game. Concentrate on only the patterns that are important for your game style.

SERVE PATTERNS

You should use the serve either to win the point straight out or to elicit a weak response that will enable you to take control of the point. The pros serve to only three basic locations: out wide, right at the body, and down the tee. The important thing is not whether you hit an ace on your serve (though it's nice if you can) but to understand the patterns of play that are started from serving to each of these three locations.

• **Serve out wide.** The objective here is to pull your opponent off the court with a short, wide serve. You can do this with accuracy, spin, or a combination of the two. In the deuce court, a right-hander would probably use a slice serve and in the ad court, probably a kick serve.

If you can pull your opponent off the court with a wide serve, then you can hit your next shot into the open court. Where that opening is may depend on where your opponent hits his return. For example, if your opponent returns down the line, hit to the open court with a crosscourt response. If your opponent returns to the middle of the court, hit to the open court again with a crosscourt shot. And if your opponent returns your wide serve crosscourt, then you have an option of hitting either down the line or back behind your opponent.

- **Serve to the body.** The objective is to jam your opponent by serving right at her, making it difficult for her to create any angles on the return. If you hit a spin serve instead of a flat one, your serve should break into your opponent's body. Because it's hard for your opponent to hit an angle on her return, her response will most often be toward the middle of the court. Your next shot should be to hit to the open court or behind your opponent.

- **Serve down the tee.** The objective in serving down the middle of the court is to make your opponent stretch to reach the ball. In the deuce court, this would necessitate a flat serve (provided you are right-handed) so that it does not break toward your opponent. In the ad court you can hit with some slice so that it breaks away from your opponent. If you serve to the tee, your opponent's most likely response is to hit the return toward the middle of the court. If he does, you have the option either to hit behind him or to the open court. One corollary advantage to serving to the tee is that this type of serve travels the shortest distance and over the lowest part of the net, which gives you a higher likelihood for making the serve and, in fact, hitting an ace.

RETURN PATTERNS

Your number one objective when returning the serve is to get the ball back in play! This is particularly important if your opponent has a big serve because you may not get many chances against it. Regardless, you should use three basic return patterns with a variety of shots.

- **Neutralize your opponent.** Hit the return deep and down the middle of the court. This can be an aggressive drive or a deep, looping shot that pushes your opponent back and doesn't allow him to attack. One variation occurs when your opponent serves and volleys. If he comes to the net behind his serve, you should neutralize his position by putting your return at his feet.

- **Attack down the line.** An effective way to attack your opponent on her serve is to take the ball early and hit down the line. This should be an aggressive shot because, if it is not hit well, your opponent will have an easy shot crosscourt to put you on the defensive.

Attacking your opponent's serve is an excellent play on the second serve. Returning down the line against a second serve is an excellent opportunity to follow your shot in to the net. Watch Pete Sampras or Andy Roddick rip a forehand return down the line and follow it to the net to finish off the point.

- **Get a high crosscourt percentage.** Hitting your return crosscourt gives you the highest-percentage shot because it gives you the biggest target area (more court, lower net) to hit the ball into play. When you hit against a big server, this return is crucial because it gives you a greater margin for error. And, if you contact the ball late, it will still go in.

BACKCOURT PATTERNS

Once the ball is in play and both you and your opponent are in the backcourt, your objective is to take control of the point. The top professionals use five primary patterns from the backcourt to take charge.

• **Rally crosscourt.** Playing the ball crosscourt is (generally) high-percentage tennis. Be consistent by hitting the ball deep with reasonable pace and good net clearance. Let your opponent make more errors by trying to change the direction of the ball or trying something fancy. Avoid breaking the crosscourt pattern unless you get a short ball or weak response that you can attack.

• **Rally crosscourt, then hit down the line.** Since most players will expect you to rally crosscourt, you can take control of the point after hitting crosscourt by changing the direction of the ball and hitting down the line. This is best done when you receive a shorter ball or your opponent is out of position. Keep in mind that most unforced errors come from this pattern because changing directions off of a crosscourt ball is a lower-percentage shot. Also be aware that the down-the-line shot often looks open when it is not because when you hit down the line the ball does not break away from your opponent.

• **Hit an angle to open up the court.** If your opponent hits a ball slightly off to the side of the court that's not too deep and sits up a little (in the creative zone), that's a perfect invitation to hit a short-angle crosscourt shot to put your opponent on the run. If you can pull your opponent off the court, your next shot should be hit deep to the open court.

• **Hit inside out.** This is one of the favorite patterns of the pros. When the ball lands in the middle of the court (in the control center), run around the ball to hit your forehand inside out to your opponent's backhand. This most often allows you to hit your strength to your opponent's weakness and makes it hard for your opponent to hit back to your backhand, giving you another forehand to hit. You can either hit to the open court or back behind your opponent, depending on where your opponent returns the ball.

• **Hit high to the backhand.** Even the pros don't like to play high backhands. So, you should loop the ball (with topspin if you can) high to your opponent's backhand. As your opponent moves back to hit the ball more comfortably, you should take a step into the court in anticipation of a short response. If his response is short enough, you can hit to the open court or behind him.

TRANSITION PATTERNS

If you want to get to the net from the backcourt, the quality of your approach shot is far more important than the pattern of play. Therefore, you should focus on placement and moving the ball through the court with enough pace or slice to keep it low. The point is that if your approach shot sits up, you are a sitting duck to be passed! Beyond the approach shot, here are the patterns you can play in the transition game when you come to the net.

• **Approach down the line.** When you hit a quality approach shot down the line and follow to the net, your opponent has few options. Your patterns depend on where your opponent hits her shot. If she goes crosscourt, volley to the open court. If she goes down the line, again volley to the open court. If she goes up the middle, you have the choice to volley to the open court or behind your opponent.

• **Approach down the middle.** When you hit your approach down the middle of the court, you usually don't have the angles to put the first volley away, but you cut down on the angles your opponent can hit to pass you. Most often you should try to set up the put-away with your next shot. So if your opponent goes down either line off your approach shot, you should volley the ball back down the line. The exception is if your opponent hits a weak shot that floats up high over the net. Then you should volley the easy sitter crosscourt. If your opponent takes your middle approach shot and goes back up the middle, you have the choice to volley to the open court or behind your opponent.

• **Sneak attack.** When you hurt your opponent by hitting either a crosscourt or down-the-line shot and stretching him out, it is highly unlikely he can hit an effective passing shot on the run. Your pattern of play is to sneak in to the net behind your shot and then volley to the open court.

> The first time I learned about the importance of a "sneak attack" was my first lesson with the great and colorful Pancho Segura. At 17 years old, I was one of the top juniors in the country. I felt as if I was hitting the ball well but needed to take my tactical understanding of the game to a new level. So, my dream was to work with the legendary Pancho Segura. Considered by many to have the best forehand (he hit it with two hands) of all time and be one of the greatest tacticians ever, Pancho was a renowned player and coach who had worked with many great players such as Jimmy Connors. Eventually I was able to make my first trip. I'll never forget that lesson. Pancho must have been in his mid-50s at the time and was about 5 feet 6 inches and very bowlegged. Not an imposing sight! We warmed up and started to play points. His serve wasn't very good, but, boy, were his ground strokes and return great. I remember running all over the court to keep up with him. After the second point, he hit an angle shot out wide to my forehand; as I was sprinting to get to the ball, he noticed my speed and said, "Hey, kid, you got great wheels!" Then as I got the ball back in play, he hit the ball to the other side. I

could hear him laughing as I ran over to the other side to hit a neutralizing ball back deep to the corner. But the next thing I saw after hitting my shot is Pancho standing at the net smiling at me as he put away the easy volley. He had surprised me by sneaking in while I was stretching for the ball! He said in his heavy accent and colorful language, "Hey, buddy, never let the SOBs you are playing feel comfortable! You see what I did? Always put pressure on them. When they think you are staying back, you sneak in. When they think you are coming in, you sometimes stay back. But any time you pull a player out wide to the backhand and you see him stretch, look to sneak into the net." I never forgot that advice, and I used it many times throughout my career. From then on, whenever I executed it well, I would always flash back to my first lesson with Pancho.

Nick Saviano and Pancho Segura at the 1986 U.S. Open.

- **From the center (inside out or crosscourt).** Many of the balls you will approach will be from the center (in the control center). In this situation, you can play the ball to either corner of the court. This is a favorite approach of the pros because the approach is moving at an angle away from their opponent, forcing them to be on the move. If the approach is hit with some pace and depth, your opponent's passing shot will usually go down the line, which should be followed up with a crosscourt volley to the open court.

SERVE-AND-VOLLEY PATTERNS

Few players at any level, including the pros, serve and volley all the time. Most often players use this tactic to throw their opponents off balance. Whether you're a Patrick Rafter clone or using the serve and volley as a change of pace against your opponent, the play patterns hold the same. The keys to an effective serve and volley are a quality serve that is well placed and a first volley that is a high-percentage shot. Where you volley most often depends on the quality and placement of the return. But basic patterns give you a higher percentage of success:

- **Serve out wide, volley to the open court.** This is a simple but effective pattern. Pull your opponent wide with the serve, and volley to the open court. If your opponent hits a good return down the line, you might be forced to keep the ball in front of you by volleying down the line and getting in position for the next shot.

- **Serve to the tee, volley behind your opponent.** Use this tactic to stretch your opponent toward the middle of the court and then volley behind him.

- **Serve to the body.** The tactic here is to elicit a weak return by "handcuffing" your opponent. Then hit the volley to her weakness or to the open court if it is available.

Sound Tactics

To make sound tactical adjustments in a match, you must have a good understanding of the factors that are affecting play and a realistic assessment of what is transpiring in the match. Great competitors—who specifically need to be good tacticians—have this skill. They know exactly what is happening on the court and ultimately figure out the best way to maximize their skills and adjust accordingly. To do this in your game, you must first be aware of the factors that influence play.

When you go to the court for competitive battle, three primary factors will affect your match

1. **You.** This includes your game and how you have prepared for the competition. You are the most important factor to success. (In fact, you can

guarantee success every time you compete. Note that I said success, not victory. There will be more on this later in chapter 8.)

2. **Your opponent.** The second biggest factor that will affect your match is the person you are playing. This includes what level of player she is; her style of game; the tactics she uses; and her strengths, weaknesses, and competitive toughness.

3. **The environment.** Factors such as the court surface, the time of day, indoors or outdoors, the wind, the sun, the temperature, the weather, crowd noise, and the like all affect your play.

Unfortunately, many players have no clue about what actually is happening on the court or why. We have all been at a tournament and heard two players come off the court and talk separately about the match they just played against each other. It's as if they had played two separate matches! The point is that often a huge gap exists between perception and reality.

TACTICAL ADJUSTMENTS

How many times have you heard coaches and teaching pros say, "Never change a winning game; always change a losing game." Good advice? Not really. How do you know your game, which has won for you in the past, is not a winner for you now? Just because you're losing doesn't mean you have the wrong tactics. Being able to tell the difference is crucial.

In tennis, change is not always good. And if you must change, subtle is better than radical. Major adjustments, especially during a match, are rarely necessary or beneficial. When a match is not going well for you, the first question to ask yourself is "Am I executing my game well?" not "What should I change?" If you are not executing your game well, then your focus should be better execution, not changing your game plan. For example, if you are an aggressive baseliner but you are losing the match because of too many unforced errors, your tactics may not be the problem. You may simply need to move your feet more or to take more time between points. By focusing on better execution in such situations, the problem can often be solved without changing your game.

If you are still struggling despite focusing on your execution, then you need to evaluate your tactics and possibly make some adjustments. Remember that subtle tactical adjustments will often make the difference, provided they are accomplished with good execution. And any adjustments you do make should always be done within the context of your basic strategy.

Here are some examples. Say a player is attacking your serve. Maybe all you need to do is vary the location of your serves a little more. Or, if your opponent is beating up on your ground strokes, perhaps a little more depth will keep him from hurting you. Aim higher over the net, and that might just do the trick. If you serve and volley and your opponent keeps passing you off your volley, it could be as simple as hitting your volleys with a little more pace.

An example of how a subtle and simple tactical adjustment can have a profound impact on a match was in the 1991 French Open men's final. Jim Courier, in his first Grand Slam final, faced countryman Andre Agassi. Agassi was winning the match two sets to one and was dominating the points on his serve. Courier was struggling just to hold his own serve. At that point, as fate would have it, the skies over Paris opened up, and it started to rain. The players left the court and, during the rain delay, were able to confer with their coaches about the match. When the delay ended and the match resumed, Courier completely turned the match around and won in five sets.

It became known that the tactical advice Courier received from his coach, Jose Higueras, changed the whole complexion of the match. What did he tell Courier to do? Did he construct a complicated and intricate tactical plan to counter what Agassi was doing? No. The only adjustment Courier made was simply to move back a few feet when returning serve to give himself more time and be more consistent getting the ball in play. That was it! Something as simple as standing farther back changed the whole match.

So when you are in the heat of competition, follow this simple protocol when things are not going well.

1. Stay with your basic game style.
2. Follow the strategy you have decided on for the match.
3. Focus on execution. If the match is not going well, evaluate your execution. Most of the time poor execution is the reason for your problems rather then poor strategy or tactics.
4. Reevaluate your tactics. If after reviewing the previous three protocols you are still struggling in the match, evaluate your tactics. They might not be appropriate against this opponent or in these conditions.
5. Make subtle tactical adjustments within the context of your strategy.
6. By this point, if you are still going down in flames, then you can try some radical tactical adjustment because you are probably going to lose anyway!

Knowledge about tactics is not going to do you much good if you do not have good perceptive skills to know what is actually happening on the court. So, sharpen your awareness of the world around you, and you'll see your ability to make good tactical adjustments expand exponentially.

Personal Tactics

First impressions are important. In competitive tennis, it is important to impose your game strategically, physically, and psychologically on your opponent as quickly as possible. It should be eminently clear to your opponent from the first game that you intend to set the tone for the match.

The pros know this very well. Look at how they start their matches. Andy Roddick and Pete Sampras will go for a blistering ace down the tee on their first serve. Andre Agassi will take the first return of serve and rip it. Lindsay Davenport will pound a ground stroke deep into the corner on the first ball. Like a deer, Venus Williams will run down the first ball you try to hit past her. Before switching sides on the first changeover, all of these great players have made an impression that is imprinted indelibly in their opponents' brains for the duration of the match. This first impression can be a very powerful tactical tool that can not only intimidate your opponent but can be used to create doubt in your opponent's mind over what shots you will hit during the match.

The great Fred Stolle once told me that, in the first game of a match when he was returning against a serve and volleyer, he would try to hit one passing shot down the line, one crosscourt, one lob, and one soft return down at the feet. By hitting all these variations, Stolle tried to create doubt in his opponent's mind as to what return he was going to hit. Then, during the match, he would hit his favorite passing shot or the most effective one most of the time.

You also can use your first impression to "bluff your opponent" to help cover weaknesses in your game. For example, if you have a weak forehand and a strong backhand, you might want to start out by taking a rip at a few forehands and bluff like it's your better side. You might be able to sucker your opponent into playing to your backhand.

By making the right first impression, you can influence the entire match tactically. Let your opponent feel your presence strategically, physically, and psychologically right from the beginning. This is one type of relationship in which it is okay to make the other person feel uncomfortable.

Variety Is the Spice of Life

Within the context of your strategy, your tactics should include some variety. Even when you are executing beautifully, if you get too predictable, your opponent will have an easier time adjusting to what you are doing. The trick is to add enough variety to keep your opponent off balance but not so much that it detracts from implementing your game plan.

Jimmy Connors was the best I ever saw at doing this. Connors was an aggressive baseliner. He basically would serve and stay back, but then, out of nowhere, he would serve and volley, sometimes on an ordinary point and at other times on a big point. From the backcourt, he played aggressive, high-percentage tennis, rarely hitting a low-percentage shot. But just when you thought you knew what he might do, he would completely surprise you by hitting a drop shot or ripping a backhand down the line and coming into the net. Against Jimmy you felt you could never get into a groove. These subtle interjections of variety were rarely mentioned or acknowledged when Connors was playing, but they are one of the reasons I consider him to be one of the best tactical players of all time.

Consider adding this type of variety to your game. With a little change of pace at the correct times, your opponent's ability to anticipate will be limited. It will create confusion and frustration that will keep your opponent off his own game. Don't only add variety on "low-anxiety" points, like at 40–0 or 0–40. Consider changing it up on pressure situations to add an element of surprise. Often the element of surprise by itself can cause your opponent to miss. And even if you don't win the point, it still serves the purpose of creating uncertainty in your opponent. Here are some specific examples for each style of game.

• **Counterpuncher**—To mix it up if you are a counterpuncher, occasionally come into the net when you have your opponent out of position. Also vary some of the patterns you play off the ground. Go for a winner on a short ball you usually would play safely. When serving, go for a big first serve sometimes. Even if you are passing your opponent at will when she comes to the net, throw in an offensive lob every once in a while to keep her from closing in too tight.

• **Aggressive baseliner**—Come to the net occasionally after a big ground stroke to keep your opponent off balance. Vary your backcourt patterns once in a while. Throw in a serve and volley at 40–0. Use an angle to open up the court. If you play the forehand inside out most of the time, surprise your opponent by ripping it crosscourt.

• **All-court player**—Because your game style is based on variety, it may not be necessary to try to change up your patterns. However, be aware of whether you have any tendencies on the court, such as preferring to pass down the line or only approaching off your backhand. Throwing in a surprise among these tendencies will be effective in keeping your opponent off balance.

• **Net rusher**—Let's say you are serving and volleying successfully in a match, serving both down the tee and out wide. This may be effective for a while, but as the match goes on your opponent is going to get a better "read" on what you are doing and respond quicker and more effectively. Simply mixing in a few body serves will help keep your opponent off balance. You might even occasionally serve and stay back. If you are coming to the net off your ground strokes, occasionally mix it up by approaching to the forehand or to the middle, as well as to the backhand.

Tactical Myths

Many players believe in myths. They think that if they can only win the seventh game of every set, they will win the match. Of course, in tennis—as in life—myths are merely misperceptions about reality. Let me dispel some tactical myths you might have heard about (or even believe!)

● *Whoever wins the big points wins the match* ●

Yes and no. The concept of big points is often overstated, overemphasized, and counterproductive. Yes, big points affect the outcome of a match, and, no, they often are not as big as you think. The add point is often referred to as a big point. Let's say I win all three add points in a match. That means I could have still lost the match 6–1, 6–2. If I am losing all of the "not so big" points, guess what—I lose! Yes, in a close match pivotal points such as 5–4, 30–40 have a significant impact on the match. And you might want to play a "big point" differently from one with less perceived pressure. For example, if I am serving with a break point against me, I generally will try to play the point into my strengths and with high-percentage shot selection. However, here is something to think about. If you get a break point and lose it, then get another break point and win it, which one was more important? Was it the first or the second break point—or was it the deuce point that got you to the break in the first place? The fact is that 99 percent of the time the player who wins the most points in a match wins the match. It's better to focus on executing one point at a time and playing that point to the best of your ability, no matter what the situation. Worry less about big points and more about executing one point at a time, and you will become a better player.

● *Always change a losing game* ●

I alluded to this earlier in the chapter, and I found that you shouldn't always change a losing game. Often it is simply a matter of improving execution. And who's to say it is a losing game plan? Your game maximizes your strengths and minimizes your weaknesses, and it may be your best chance to win. In addition, maybe your opponent has hit a hot streak, or you've had a run of misfortune. It may be a matter of sticking to your game and imposing your plan on the match.

● *Never change a winning game* ●

This is a semi-myth. If you're winning, you don't want to change your game per se, but you better have some variety in the patterns you play. Otherwise, chances are your opponent will start to catch on to what you are doing and begin to get better at countering it.

● *You have to outthink your opponent* ●

More often than not, imposing your strategy on your opponent and executing it well determine a match. Yes, many times you need to adjust to what your opponent is doing during a match, but this concept is overemphasized. Given two players at the same level who use basic, sound tactics, who wins usually comes down to execution, control of your emotions, and minor tactical adjustments. Tennis is not a game of chess. It is more analogous to a game of checkers. I think more matches are lost from thinking too much than are won by outthinking an opponent.

● *You have to raise your level of play in a tiebreaker* ●

This myth implies that you were not playing at your best or not maximizing your concentration before the tiebreaker. I don't agree with this mentality. Agassi once said: "When I am playing my best I play every point like it is a tiebreaker." When players are at their best, they focus on one point at a time and play each point to the best of their ability regardless of the score or situation. Having said that, I like players to play aggressive, yet high-percentage tennis in a tie-breaker situation where they play their strengths as much as possible.

● *You have to win the all-important seventh game* ●

This is one of the most ridiculous beliefs I have ever heard in sports. Is the seventh game at 5–1 more important than at 5–4 or 5–6? Give me a break!

● *Always approach down the line* ●

Do this only if you want your opponent standing on the line waiting to pass you. That's what would happen if everyone believed that myth. There are times to approach crosscourt, up the middle, or inside out. And I've discussed the importance of changing things up to keep your game from becoming predictable and to keep your opponent off balance.

● *Always volley to the open court* ●

It depends on how open the court is. Other factors come into play, as well. If you're playing a real speed burner, especially on clay, you may want to hit your volley behind your opponent to wrong-foot him. The height of the ball may dictate not going for the winner but putting the ball deep right at your opponent to set up the next volley.

● *When you are up a break, just concentrate on holding your serve* ●

Nonsense! Of course you want to hold serve, but why give up the aggressive play that earned you the lead? Just as at all other times, you should continue to focus on just one point at a time. Maybe you can break a second or third time.

Countering Different Game Styles

One point transcends every game style and strategy regardless of whom you are playing. Your number-one goal strategically and tactically is to impose your game on your opponent by highlighting your strengths as much as possible and minimizing your weaknesses. The fatal mistake that players make is to fall into the trap of playing the other player's style of game. For example, if you are playing a counterpuncher the last thing you want to try is to beat him at his own game, unless you are a counterpuncher. Remember, play your game, do what you do best, and make the necessary subtle tactical adjustments. Stay true to the player you are!

If you remember one thing about this chapter, it should be that your tactics must emanate from your strategy! Yes, you need to know and use basic principles of high-percentage, sound shot selection and other areas discussed in this chapter. But never, never lose sight of the type of player you are. Within that context, make the necessary tactical adjustments you need to make during competition. If you follow this simple principle, I promise you your tactical prowess on the court will take you to the next level without even hitting the ball any better than you do now. If you combine this newfound knowledge with the advice from the next chapter on optimizing technique, well, the sky is the limit!

CHAPTER 4

Optimize Technique

> "Focusing on the true fundamentals of technique will allow your natural hitting style to emerge, enabling you to hit cleanly, consistently, and with power."

No standard technique or swing path for a stroke exists that is optimum for all players. However, there is an optimum technique for each individual player. Every player is unique, with her own individual physical and psychological characteristics. What is optimum for one player, therefore, may not be optimum for another. That is why the world-class professionals in the game today use a variety of techniques.

Good technique is one of the keys to success in tennis; optimum technique is a key to reaching your full potential. The secret to optimizing your technique is to focus on fundamentals of the game, while letting your own natural hitting style and flair evolve.

Patrick McEnroe

Captain of the United States Davis Cup Team and former world-class player

People ask me all the time that if I were to teach a kid how to play or take a junior and mold their strokes, what would I want their technique to be. Should they hit with heavy spin or flatter strokes? Extreme grips or more traditional? A one or two-handed backhand? My answer to these questions, and any dealing with all the variables that go into building a player's game, is always the same. It's entirely based on each individual player. I feed them a ball, don't say a word, see how they naturally hit, and then work within those parameters. It's always best to take the natural instincts of the player, both mentally and physically, and let that determine their style of play. When a coach tries to impose a certain technique on a player that doesn't come naturally, it's never going to be a reliable stroke.

A stroke is like a fingerprint—no two are exactly alike and there's more than one way to hit on. In this chapter Nick shows you the most efficient and effective foundations on which to build your strokes. He starts with the idea of getting yourself in proper position and being balanced when you do swing—core elements to getting into an optimal hitting zone. With these fundamental pieces in place you will develop your own technique that will make you comfortable with your strokes. If you're comfortable, then you're confident. That is absolutely crucial when it comes to executing your strokes under pressure on a consistent basis. If you don't feel good about your swing, then your technique won't be sound, and when the match gets tight your stroke will desert you.

My older brother, John, is a great example of letting a player flourish with his instinctive techniques. He obviously had his own unique style of play. In today's game you would hardly see anyone trying to play with one grip like he did. Even though many of his strokes don't look like they've been pulled from a textbook, if you analyze the elements like taking the ball early, being balanced, and hitting through the shot, they're almost perfect. They worked because his fundamentals were so sound. As long as your foundations are solid, then your own individuality can surface and come through in your strokes. That's what it takes to be an effective ball striker. Focus on the fundamentals discussed throughout this chapter; they will provide you with a clear guide to developing your strokes to their full potential.

Understanding the Fundamentals of Technique

A great deal of confusion exists as to what fundamentals of technique are. The secret is to be able to differentiate between critical mechanical fundamentals and individualistic styles of hitting, while eliminating technical flaws that limit your ability. The beautiful thing about knowing the fundamentals is that by working on them you will naturally eliminate most of the technical flaws. So this chapter will focus on simply what I consider to be the key technical fundamentals on ground strokes, volleys, returns, and serves. These fundamentals are relevant and applicable to virtually all ages and levels of play. You can pick out any stroke, learn the main points, work on them, and your game will improve.

Unfortunately, many players—from club players right up to touring professionals—spend most of their time working on the wrong technical things. They often attempt to correct technical flaws by working on their hitting style, which they mistakenly confuse with fundamental technique. This is an act of futility if the player does not possess the fundamentals in the first place.

For example, a player with poor body position in relation to the ball when she hits her two-handed backhand who spends her time working on the type of backswing she is going to take—loop or straight back—is engaging in an act of futility. Great players hit with many types of backswings successfully. However, no one with a great two-handed backhand hits with consistently poor body position in relation to the ball. The type of backswing is more a style of hitting; good body position is a fundamental. Remember, the fundamentals I will talk about in this chapter transcend style of hitting.

Look at the forehands of Pete Sampras, Venus Williams, and Andy Roddick (see photos page 70). These great players all have very different techniques on their forehands. Each has a unique style of hitting the ball. Yet all three execute the basic fundamentals of the stroke flawlessly. The question is, do you know what those fundamentals are?

Once you know the true fundamentals of technique, you can turn your efforts to improving them. And when you do, two wonderful things will happen. First, you will improve the foundation of your technique, and, second, your personal style and flair on the court will emerge naturally. This combination is the key to developing your optimum technique, which will dramatically improve your game and maximize your enjoyment, as well.

Pete Sampras, Venus Williams, and Andy Roddick demonstrate the forehand.
© Lance Jeffrey

Development as a Whole

You must look at developing your technique as part of a whole process of developing your ability to play the game successfully. Having good technique should not be your ultimate goal. It also cannot be taught in a vacuum. What I mean by that is that you don't want to constantly separate your technique work from your tactics of play. Too many players think that improving their technique will solve all of their problems. Your objective, therefore, is to develop your optimum technique that will enhance your strategy, tactics, shot selection, and ability to play points in a match.

Years ago, a young female pro I was working with called me at 2:00 A.M. from Europe in a panic. "Nick," she cried on the phone, "I am missing all my backhands in the middle of the net. What should I do?" Obviously, she was looking for some profound technical advice. Tired, and not a little annoyed, I simply told her, "Aim higher!" and hung up. Later on when I spoke with her, she said that my advice really helped. The point is that having good technique means very little if it is not viewed as just another component of playing the game.

A few years ago, I spoke at the International Tennis Federation Worldwide Coaching workshop in Casablanca. There were 300 top developmental coaches from 70 countries in attendance. During my talk, the audience became extremely quiet when I said, "If you are teaching your players to imitate the techniques of the top players in the game today, you are teaching them to be a generation behind the next wave of champions."

I immediately had everyone's attention. I explained that high-performance coaches should not focus on hitting style but on the true mechanical fundamentals of technique. The true fundamentals are generally the commonalities in technique and movement that virtually all great players execute. In addition, during practice, they (coaches) must simulate the demands their players will encounter at the world-class level. This will allow the players' technical fundamentals to be honed to adapt to the ever-changing demands of the game, while their style of hitting evolves naturally in accordance with their personality and physical attributes. This combination creates optimum technique.

I continued by saying that the game is evolving constantly. Players from one generation do not have the same technique as those of the past. (Just look at the progression of male world champions, from Jimmy Connors and Bjorn Borg of the 1970s; to John McEnroe, Boris Becker, and Stefan Edberg in the 1980s; to Jim Courier, Pete Sampras, and Andre Agassi in the 1990s. The same is true for women, with Billie Jean King to Chris Evert; to Martina Navratilova; to Steffi Graf; to Monica Seles; to Martina Hingis, Lindsay Davenport, and Venus and Serena Williams today. As a coach, I don't want to limit players to antiquated techniques and hitting styles that do not allow them to develop to their full potential. So, if you want to develop the next great champion, remember, that player will probably look different—technically speaking—from the champions of today.

For example, you don't want to work your backhand slice only by having someone feed you balls in practice (assuming you are not learning the slice for the first time). You need to incorporate tactical situations into your practice. You not only need to learn how to hit the shot but when to hit it, as well as from different locations and in different match situations. It's a lot different hitting a slice when you want to approach the net than trying to keep the ball low against an opponent who is rushing the net. So, when you are working on technique, always attempt to incorporate the tactical element into the session.

I remember when I first realized that the game (and technique in particular) were evolving. I was playing in a tour event in Germany in 1983 in a first-round doubles match. We were playing against two juniors 15 and 16 years old from Germany, and we were hanging on for dear life as these two young players were pounding the ball at us. It was a packed house, and the crowd was going crazy because these two young Germans were part of their elite national team and there were high hopes for them. I remember thinking, *Here I am, a veteran touring professional, having trouble handling the pace of a 15-year-old. Wow, how the game has changed. It must be time for me to retire!* Well, we barely beat them 7–5 in the third set. However, the good news was that we went on to win the tournament, so the thought about retirement was forgotten. But that young 15-year-old was not forgotten. His name is Boris Becker! Boris, along with Ivan Lendl, helped to revolutionize pro tennis with the power game.

Characteristics of Great Technique

Richard Schonborn of Germany—one of the top high-performance coaches in the world and a friend of mine—says that great technique has three characteristics (see his book, *Advanced Techniques for Competitive Tennis*). I have expanded his ideas to five characteristics of great technique.

1. **Simple.** It uses only the necessary (or few) body parts as possible and contains no unnecessary or counterproductive movements.
2. **Efficient.** It uses a minimum of effort to accomplish the objective. It also helps to minimize stress to the body, which can prevent injury.
3. **Effective.** It produces the desired results with consistency.
4. **Flexible and versatile.** It can be adapted to the tactical requirements of match situations.
5. **Compatible.** It facilitates your ability to play the game consistent with your personality.

Remember your objective is to optimize your technique by learning the mechanical fundamentals of stroke production and allowing for your own individual stroke characteristics (your style) to evolve.

Back to Basics

In the following paragraphs, I have listed key points that are applicable to almost every stroke. (The serve is an exception in a few cases because some of the mechanics of the serve apply only to that shot.) Regardless of your level of play—whether you are a beginner or a world-class professional—these fundamentals transcend every style and level of ability.

BALANCE AND CENTER OF GRAVITY

One of the single biggest causes of errors in tennis is poor balance. Your balance is interconnected with your center of gravity. Think of balance as your ability to control your equilibrium or stability. There are two types of balance. *Static balance* is the ability to control the body while the body is not moving (for example, when you are about to serve). *Dynamic balance* is the ability to control the body during motion (for example, when you change direction after hitting a shot or when hitting on the run).

Your center of gravity constantly moves as you play. It is an imaginary point around which your body weight is evenly distributed. The ideal position as you are preparing to split step or to execute a shot is to have a low center of gravity (accomplished by bending the knees), with the center of gravity located directly above a point in between your feet or what is called your base. This concept is critical in understanding balance and stability and how gravity affects your tennis techniques.

(a) Lleyton Hewitt displays a low center of gravity distributed over his base as he lands from his split step. *(b)* Hewitt maintains good upper body posture as he approaches the ball. *(c)* Note Hewitt's form—beautiful balance, good posture, wide base of support, knees bent, head pointed at hitting zone.
© Lance Jeffrey

a   b   c

For optimum stroke production, here are the key fundamentals relating to balance and center of gravity that you should focus on.

- **Keep good upper-body posture:** Keep your head up and your shoulders and back relatively straight, as you approach and contact the ball.
- **Keep your upper body still:** Attempt to keep your upper body still with minimal movement of your head in particular as you move to the ball.
- **Keep your head still:** During the preparation phase and pointed in the direction of the hitting zone during the hitting phase keep your head as still as you can.
- **Use a proper base of support:** Keep your feet at least shoulder-width apart as you set up to prepare to hit the ball.
- **Enhance stability:** During the preparation phase and backswing, bend your knees, which will lower your center of gravity and enhance stability.

KINETIC CHAIN

Don't be scared off by the fancy name. Kinetic chain simply means that the body acts as a system of chain links, whereby the force generated by one part of the body is transferred smoothly to the next. Think of it this way: Your body coils in the preparation phase by rotation of your shoulders, trunk, hips, and bending your knees. Then your body uncoils during the hitting stage, with the energy being transferred up from your legs to your hips, trunk, shoulders, arm, wrist, and finally to your racket. This is how the pros generate so much power.

It is important that you at least understand the concept that the most powerful tennis strokes (serves and ground strokes) begin with a leg drive that generates ground reaction forces that can be transferred up the segments of the kinetic chain to the racket. This knowledge will help you better understand how to analyze your own technique and subsequently what you need to work on.

GRIPS

Four major types of grips are used in tennis: continental, eastern, semiwestern, and western. Each has advantages and disadvantages. The type of grip used will also affect a player's game style and tactics.

- **Continental.** The continental grip is one of the most common grips for the volley and the serve. It is not commonly used for forehand ground strokes, but many players—including world-class players—use it for both one- and two-handed backhands. The most effective hitting zone for the

(a) James Blake demonstrates kinetic chain by loading the large muscle groups in the preparation phase, *(b)* then unleashing this energy from the ground up.
© Lance Jeffrey

continental grip tends to be lower and slightly closer to the body than the hitting zone for the eastern grip. When three out of the four Grand Slam tournaments were played on grass, many pros used the continental grip for both the forehand and backhand because of the extremely low bounce on grass. Few do today. If you are a young, aspiring player and you use this grip for the forehand, I recommend that you get in touch with a local U.S. Professional Tennis Association (USPTA) or Professional Tennis Registry (PTR) pro to help you change it to an eastern grip.

Advantages of the continental grip are that it is effective for both the backhand and forehand volleys thereby eliminating the need to change your grip at the net; and it is effective for serving because it allows for good wrist action and forearm pronation. However, disadvantages of using the continental grip include difficulty in hitting medium to high balls and generating even a small amount of topspin on the forehand side.

- **Eastern.** The classic eastern forehand and backhand grip is suitable for all spins and stances. It has a comfortable hitting zone that is slightly higher and farther in front than the continental hitting zone. The eastern grip is now a common grip for the one-handed backhand. Advantages of using the eastern grip are that it is effective for most types of shots, including drives and topspin, and it has few significant limitations. One disadvantage is the difficulty in using it on balls at shoulder height or higher.

- **Semiwestern.** This grip is used for the forehand. By rotating the hand clockwise from the eastern grip, the semiwestern grip allows you to hit balls that bounce higher more comfortably and facilitates the use of topspin. This is a common grip among top professionals. The most comfortable hitting zone for the semiwestern grip is between chest and shoulder height. Advantages of using the semiwestern grip are that it is good for imparting topspin, hitting with power, and dealing with balls that are above waist height. Some disadvantages include difficulty in handling balls that are below waist level and short balls that land close to the net, and having a larger grip change from forehand to standard backhand grips.

> When Bjorn Borg first burst onto the international scene by winning the Italian and French Open championships as a teenager, he used the semiwestern grip. This grip was considered so incredibly extreme that all of the so-called experts confidently predicted that he could win only on clay because the ball bounced up high and he would never be able to adjust to grass-court tennis where the bounce was low. Well, after winning five consecutive Wimbledon championships (played on grass), nobody said that anymore. Now the semiwestern grip is the most common grip on the pro tour for the forehand.

- **Western.** The western grip rotates farther around than the semiwestern and places the hand beneath the grip. This grip is not to be used for backhands and is considered an extreme grip even for forehands. Many professionals use this grip, most often clay-court specialists, because the ball bounces higher on clay. I would not recommend this grip for young players because it can limit the development of a well-rounded game. Players who use the western grip often have difficulty transitioning to the net and hitting volleys. Advantages of the western grip include being good for imparting topspin on medium to high bouncing balls and making it easy to deal with balls at chest height or higher. A few disadvantages are the extreme difficulty in dealing with balls that are below waist level and short balls that land close to the net; causing problems for hitting forehands on the run; having a large grip change from forehand to standard backhand grips; and having difficulty developing a well-rounded game. Players who use this grip often have difficulty making the adjustment to using the continental grip for volleys.

Preparing Your Stroke

You can have the prettiest-looking strokes in the world, but if you don't have sound fundamentals in moving to the ball and preparing to hit it, the rest of your stroke is a crapshoot. Good preparation will not only allow you to maximize control and power, it is also critical in enabling you to cope with the increased power in the game today.

Ground Strokes

The fundamental techniques in preparing to hit a shot are the split step; the unit turn; movement to the ball (or tracking); racket preparation, and stroke patterns. If you improve any or all of these areas, your level of play will improve considerably.

(a) Serena Williams just landing from the split step, *(b)* starting the unit turn, *(c)* and in the initial stage of preparing her racket and tracking the ball. Note how little she has moved the racket independently up to this point.

© Lance Jeffrey

SPLIT STEP

The split step is a vitally important technique a player uses to get her body in position to move to the ball in any direction as quickly as possible and it is one of the most basic fundamentals of movement on the tennis court. A detailed explanation of how to perform a split step is in chapter 5 on movement.

UNIT TURN AND INITIAL RACKET PREPARATION

The unit turn is generally the first move players make as they come out of the split step. The leg closest to where the ball has been hit turns and steps out in the direction of the ball while the upper body (shoulders and hips) begins to rotate. Contrary to what is often taught, you do not want to take your racket back at this stage. However, the rotation of the shoulders along with a slight move back of the elbow of your racket arm contribute to the initial racket preparation.

MOVEMENT TO THE BALL OR TRACKING

After the split step and unit turn, your movement to the ball as you prepare to hit and after your recovery step to get back into position for the next shot is what I call "tracking" the ball. The key here is to maintain good posture—shoulders and back relatively straight with a slight bend forward at the waist—with minimal movement of your upper body and head. If you lose your dynamic balance and/or allow your shoulders and head wobble or bob up and down excessively, it makes it almost impossible to track the oncoming ball properly. Also, good posture gives you the freedom physically to hit whatever stroke is necessary. A common mistake is to bend over excessively at the waist, which destroys your balance and restricts your ability to produce a quality stroke. As if you were a fashion model, think of balancing a book on your head as you move to the ball.

• **Muscle loading.** I know you have probably been told a thousand times just to turn sideways when you hit the ball. But that is not enough because it will not produce adequate stretch—storing of energy in the large-muscle groups as you prepare to hit the ball. Focus on rotating your shoulders and bending at the knees. In actuality, you will be stretching or loading the large muscle groups—chest, shoulders, torso, hips, legs—without even realizing it as you prepare to hit the ball. (Refer to picture *a* on page 75 and the pictures on return of serve on *a* and *b* on page 86 for examples of this.) This is absolutely critical to maximizing your ground strokes and return of serves particularly when a ball is hit at you with great speed.

When you rotate your shoulders, you want to feel the "pull" in your front shoulder. This is an important part of your racket preparation because, once you get this "load," you'll automatically have taken about half your backswing with minimal movement of your racket arm. Loading your muscles in this manner will also enable you to generate a great deal of power with a relatively short backswing. Here is a tip to help you accomplish this. To get a feel for the loading of your upper body, have someone feed you an easy ball. Before you step across to the ball, turn your upper body and bend your knees to prepare. You will immediately feel the loading process in your major muscle groups. Refer again to page 75 (*a*) for muscle-loading photos. Page 80 illustrates excellent examples of players getting the pull in their shoulders.

RACKET PREPARATION

As you're preparing your racket consider the following: backswing, stance, and hitting zone.

• **Backswing.** It is a myth that a player should take his racket back first when he prepares to hit the ball. The point in time at which your hitting arm actually starts taking the racket back varies with different styles of racket preparation. However, the racket usually does not move independently for significant distance until much of your rotation process is completed. Technically, the elbow of your racket arm on the forehand will make a slight move back as your shoulder and hip rotation begins; however, it should feel as if your shoulders and hips are the only things turning at that time.

Backswings vary tremendously from player to player. You can take the racket relatively straight back, in a large loop, in a small loop, lead with your elbow, or use other motions. These are generally functions of style, not fundamentals; therefore, they won't be dealt with here. The main thing is to avoid extremes and to get a good rotation of your upper body.

• **Stance.** Three basic types of stances for all tennis strokes are open, squared, and closed. There has been a significant shift in the game toward the open stance on both the forehand and backhand. Here is a brief explanation of each.

1. **Open stance.** The open stance is now the most commonly used footwork with the forehand and is becoming increasingly more common on the backhand side, as well. To execute an open-stance ground stroke, line up your back leg close to the flight of the ball, with your front leg farther away and shoulders square to the net, as opposed to hitting the ball in a squared or closed stance with your shoulders turned perpendicular to the net and your feet lined up with the flight of the ball. Using an open stance saves about a half step and makes for a quicker recovery. In addition, you can get more upper-body rotation with an open stance, which gives you more power. The open stance is used on the backhand more often by two-handers, but it is growing in popularity with one-handers, as well.

2. **Squared stance.** In a squared stance, your front and back legs are perpendicular to the net. Weight is transferred forward in the direction of the hit as you step into the shot. This stance is excellent for balance and hitting a controlled shot.

3. **Closed stance.** In a closed stance, your front leg steps across your back leg so that your body is at an angle toward the side fence. A closed stance should not be used to hit a forehand, particularly with an eastern, semiwestern, or western grip. It is usually only effective on the backhand side, and your first preference should always be to use the squared stance if possible.

During the course of a match you will probably use all three stances. What stance you use on a given stroke will depend on your personal technique and the specific shot you are hitting. The point is to learn to use the stance that will help you to maximize your shot.

(a) Serena Williams hits a backhand with an open stance. (b) Lindsay Davenport hits a backhand with the classic squared stance. (c) Gustavo Kuerten hits a one-handed backhand with a closed stance. Notice the rotation and loading of the shoulders in all three players.
© Lance Jeffrey

- **Hitting zone.** The hitting zone is the distance away from your body that the ball is contacted. To develop consistent strokes, you need to establish your optimum hitting zone and consistently hit the ball in that zone. The actual contact point (how far out in front of your body you contact the ball) will vary depending on the type of shot being hit. However, your hitting zone should vary as little as possible. Basically, it should be a comfortable distance from your body that allows you to freely execute the shot. Remember, getting your body in the ideal location to contact the ball is the key objective of good footwork.

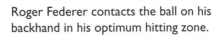

Kim Clijsters contacts the ball on her forehand in the optimum hitting zone.

Roger Federer contacts the ball on his backhand in his optimum hitting zone.

© Lance Jeffrey

© Lance Jeffrey

STROKE PATTERNS

The position of the racket head at contact is the most important element in a stroke. For most ground strokes, the racket face at impact will be very close to vertical, give or take a few degrees. Adding spin to the ball has more to do with the path the racket takes through the swing than with the opening or closing of the racket head.

For the standard drive or topspin ground stroke, the basic swing path of your racket is a low-to-high, or upward, movement through the hitting zone. The more topspin you want, the more extreme the low-to-high swing path. Some pros have as much as a 50-degree angle on their upward swing. Generating a lot of topspin requires a great deal of racket acceleration upward through the hitting zone.

A high-to-low, or downward, racket motion through impact creates backspin or slice on ground strokes. You should start out slightly above the flight of the oncoming ball and swing in a downward and out path toward your target. Even though you might open the racket face significantly as you prepare to hit and on the follow-through for the slice, at impact the racket face is only slightly open.

Vince Spadea hits his forehand with low-to-high swing path movement in order to generate topspin.
© Lance Jeffrey

a   b   c

Justin Gimelstob displays a high-to-low swing path for the slice backhand.
© Lance Jeffrey

Follow-Through

The development of new racket technology and the evolution of technique (grip changes, more spin, and the quest for maximum power) have increased racket-head speed on all shots, which has profoundly affected the follow-through and how it is taught. The most important thing to remember about the follow-through is that, if you have a good swing path leading up to and through the hitting zone, the follow-through should come naturally. In short, it is the angle and the trajectory of the racket head at impact that technically affect where the ball goes.

The ball is on the strings for only about four milliseconds, which means it is long gone before you complete even a fraction of the follow-through. So, it stands to reason that the follow-through is not really important to the stroke or shot, right? Wrong! The follow-through is an important component on all strokes.

The follow-through is a great gauge to determine whether or not you are approaching the ball with the correct swing path for the stroke you are hitting. For example, players often say that to get topspin you must get over the top of or cover the ball as you hit. Actually, you are not getting over the top of the ball on the hit but are turning over the racket face slightly after the hit as you follow through. But, by having this perception in your mind of covering the ball on the hit, it could actually be helping you to establish the correct swing path for the shot. So, even though the follow-through is not directly affecting the flight of the ball, it is in fact affecting the way you approach the ball.

A good follow-through also helps to prevent injury by minimizing strain on your arm and shoulder. Here are a few suggestions:

- After accelerating through the hitting zone on a ground stroke, don't try to stop or slow down the follow-through but rather allow it to elongate in a natural way. Often this will result in the follow-through wrapping around the neck. Having a longer distance to slow down the racket in the follow-through prevents strain on your arm and shoulder. The old teaching adage of hit and hold the finish out in front, in most cases, does not apply.

- When learning a new stroke or correcting a problem off the ground or at the net, keep these tips in mind. Keeping the racket face in the correct swing path for an extended distance after contact will increase the chance of making an accurate shot. This holds true for volleys, as well as ground strokes. Another tip is to extend your follow-through through the hitting zone and out toward the target area before allowing it to wrap around. Both of these tactics will help you learn to control the racket head through the critical hitting zone. Under normal circumstances, the follow-through will be more violent, going in and out of the hitting zone very quickly. However, if you are having trouble controlling the ball, these tips will help.

Return of Serve

The return is a hugely important shot in anyone's game, yet it is one of the least practiced shots. Remember, every point includes a return of serve (unless there is a double fault or ace), which makes it the second most important shot in the game. Improving your return technique will pay big dividends. Here are a few of the keys to hitting returns well. These points are applicable to both forehand and backhand returns.

- **Split step.** Start your split step right before your opponent strikes the ball. Focus on when contact is made to track the ball.
- **Front shoulder.** Think in terms of a quick turn of your front shoulder to rotate your upper body. Technically, other things will be happening, but you don't need to worry about them. A quick loading of the upper body will enable you to take a short backswing yet still generate power on your return.
- **Compact backswing.** Often this will happen naturally if you get a quick turn of your front shoulder. The harder the serve, the smaller the backswing.
- **Footwork.** Your objective is to hit the ball in your optimum hitting zone by moving your feet. Try to keep your feet underneath you, as opposed to stretching for the ball. If you attempt to use your feet to

a

b

a

b

Note the quick turn of the shoulders and compact backswing as Agassi prepares to hit a backhand return and Hingis hits a forehand return.
© Lance Jeffrey

get to the ball without reaching, you will move your feet more quickly and stay on balance. If the ball is far away or coming quickly, you will automatically stretch out to reach for it. The idea is that you don't want to reach for the ball unless absolutely necessary.

• **Swing.** If you take the serve early, you should feel like you are swinging through the flight of the ball, as opposed to swinging up (even though you will technically be swinging from low to high). There is less upward action on your swing because the ball is bouncing upward quickly from the ground.

I was at the practice courts at the All England Club during the first week of the 2001 Wimbledon championships, when Andre Agassi came up and sat right by me as he was waiting for his practice court. We started chatting, and I took the opportunity to show him an article on return of serve that I had written in our *USTA High Performance Coaching Newsletter* (of which I am an editor), which goes out to 25,000 coaches. The article featured a set of sequence pictures of Andre hitting a backhand return. After studying the pictures, his response stood out in my mind. He said, "Nick, I don't even think about taking the racket back. All I think about is keeping the racket in close to my body and turning my shoulders ... the technique has got to be simple!" Considering that he has one of the greatest returns of all time, I thought I would share that bit of advice with you.

Tim Henman prepares to hit a backhand volley.
© Lance Jeffrey

Roger Federer executes a forehand volley. Federer displays beautiful, simple, technique.
© Lance Jeffrey

Volleys

The secret to great technique on the volley is simplicity. Most important is the ability to move to the ball, on balance, with a minimal backswing and the ability to control the racket face at impact. The more moving parts and the bigger the swing on the volley, the harder it is to master the stroke. Unlike on ground strokes, there is not as much variation in technique on the volley among the top professionals.

• **Prepare your racket first and then move.** When you are setting up for the volley, think in terms of preparing your racket first and then moving to the ball. In fact, you will be moving and preparing the racket at the same time. However, lining up your racket early gives a clear gauge as to exactly where you need to move to get in the best position for the shot. Too many players see the ball, start to move toward it, and then try to prepare their racket. The result is poor body position in relation to the ball and trouble preparing the racket in time.

• **Maintain good posture.** Throughout the preparation and hitting phases, keep your shoulders and back relatively straight.

• **Keep your elbow bent.** As you prepare your racket for the volley, make sure your elbow is bent. You should never have a straight arm in the preparation phase of the volley.

- **Hold the racket head above your wrist**. As you prepare for the volley, your racket head generally will start well above your wrist, with the racket face slightly open.

- **Turn your upper body on the backhand.** Do not start a backhand volley with your whole body turned sideways. Facing the ball, rotate your upper body as you prepare, getting a pull in the shoulders for the strength you need on the shot, then step. This will help load the large-muscle groups of your upper body.

- **Keep your elbow out on the forehand.** Keep your elbow bent and slightly out in front of your body as you prepare for a forehand volley.

- **Use a compact swing.** Yes, the pros often take a big swing at the ball, but every great volleyer can execute either the forehand or the backhand with minimal backswing and follow-through.

Many years ago (I must have been 14) at the Berkley Tennis Club, they held a big professional men's event. My idol Rod Laver, two-time Grand Slam winner, was competing in the event. So, I went to the tournament three days in a row to watch him play. I wanted to find some time when I could ask him about his technique on the volley, but it was impossible to get near him when he was at the courts. However, I noticed that he would actually walk to the courts from his hotel, which was close to the tennis club. So on Friday, before his quarterfinal match, I got to the club early and waited outside so that I could "intercept" him on the street as he was walking to the courts. As he approached, I got really nervous. But I managed to spit it out. "Mr. Laver, can I ask you a quick question?" "Go head if you keep walking," he said. "I am trying to improve my volleys. Is there anything you can tell me that might help?" He held his racket up as if he were going to hit a forehand volley and said, "Keep the racket work simple, and be aggressive with your feet. That is when I volley my best." At first I didn't fully understand, but I never forgot what he said. As I practiced my volley and improved it over the years, it became more and more clear how right he was. To this day, the concept of simple racket technique with good movement to the ball is part of my technical philosophy on the volley. About 25 years later, I had the privilege of riding with Rod in the courtesy car at the U.S. Open. I mentioned the story to him. He remembered the tournament but not the young boy asking him about the volley. The important thing is I didn't forget!

- **Control the racket face before and after the hit.** If you can control the racket face before and slightly after the hit (if you control it before and after the hit, it means you have maintained control on contact), then you have a great chance of consistently hitting the volley well. With this in mind, in the preparation phase, attempt to line up the racket face directly behind the flight of the oncoming ball. In reality, you might be slightly higher than the oncoming ball, depending on the shot, but the key is to line it up quickly and not turn the racket face away from the oncoming ball. Then focus on keeping the face of your racket facing the direction of your target after you make contact, and hold this for a split second. This will help to keep your racket face pointed in the right direction throughout the hitting zone. It will also help minimize the size of your backswing and follow-through. All great volleyers can do this at will. So, don't be confused when you see some of the pros taking a big swing or flipping their racket head around on the follow-through.

Serve

The serve is the most important shot in the game. Every point starts with it, and it is the only shot in tennis in which you have total control over how you execute it. To say you should practice first and second serves is an understatement! I could write an entire chapter on technique for the serve. Short of doing that, I have selected a few of the most important points on technique. Once again, if you improve any one of the following items, you will help your serve significantly.

- **Relax.** The serve is liquid power. In particular, make sure there is little tension in your face or racket arm.
- **Balance.** Be balanced at the start.
- **Front toe.** Start with your front foot turned to the side (at least a 30 percent angle from the net), or it should turn as you rotate your shoulders. If your toe points directly toward the net, your ability to turn your hips and shoulders will be limited.
- **Tossing arm.** Toss the ball with your arm to the side of your body, approximately at a 45-degree angle, as opposed to straight out in front of you. This will create a natural rotation of your shoulders without thinking about it.
- **Toss location.** The location of the toss will vary from player to player according to her style. However, the toss should be slightly out in front of your body and directly above your hitting shoulder. On spin serves, it usually will be tossed a few inches over your head.
- **Toss height.** The height of your toss should be slightly higher than where you would contact the ball at full extension. A low toss will limit your power and service percentage.

Andy Roddick's powerful serve.
© Lance Jeffrey

- **Shoulders.** As you toss the ball up, you should rotate your shoulders and start to bend your knees. Rotating your shoulders at the start, along with having your tossing arm to the side of your body and your toe pointed to the side, will naturally cause a slight rotation in your hips without thinking about it.

- **Power position.** If you can get into a good power position right before exploding up, then your chances of having a good serve are excellent (photo *b* above). The power position for the serve is when your body is fully loaded (storing of energy) in your shoulders, hips, and knees right before exploding up. Your shoulders are rotated and tilted, your hips are rotated and forward, and your knees are bent. Most club players don't get into this position. However, just a mental picture of it will help your serve.

- **Head up.** Keep your head up through contact with the ball.

- **Vertical explosion.** Think of the serve as a vertical explosion, and feel like you are exploding up into the shot.

- **Breathe out.** Breathe out on the hit. It creates tension and a loss of power when you hold your breath on the hit.

"Practice your serve every day and use targets. Remember, it's the most important shot in the game." I have said that literally thousands of times to young, aspiring players. But only a few really follow that advice. Greg was one of the few who took my advice to heart. He used to fly down from Canada to work with me when he was 12 to 14 years old. "I want to be a serve and volleyer," he would say. The only thing was he was very small, and although he had developed a nice service action, I didn't think it would amount to a really significant shot. Nevertheless, he would practice it every day. Then when I took the national coaching job with the U.S. Tennis Association, I could no longer work with players from other countries. So, Greg stopped coming to my house. But we remained friends, and I would continue to see him from time to time at the top international junior events, playing matches or out on the practice courts. Each time I would see him, two things stood out. He was bigger and stronger, and his serve was getting bigger and better. I noticed that at all his practice sessions he finished the session by hitting a basket of serves with targets. Eventually, he turned professional and moved to England and started rapidly moving up the rankings, with a serve rated as one of the best in the game—clocked at more than 140 miles per hour—and a fine volley to back it up. Finally, a few years ago, as I watched him play, I marveled at the power and accuracy of 6'4" Greg Rusedski, serving and volleying his way to the finals of the U.S. Open and a top-five world ranking. Sometimes it pays to listen, and it definitely pays to practice your serve!

Greg Rusedski (far left) at 14 years old. (He grew up to be 6'4" tall.)

The secret to developing and mastering optimum technique is truly rooted in the fundamentals. As you begin to optimize your technique, don't try to work on a lot of different things at once. Check with a local certified USPTA or PTR professional, and choose one or possibly two things to focus on in an area that needs improving. If you keep it simple, focus your efforts on mastering fundamentals, and let your natural personality and style come through, you will be on your way to major improvements in your technique in particular and your game in general.

Let Movement Flow

> " Efficient movement has as much to do with the right mental approach as it does with technique. Use your subconscious mind to make court movement automatic. "

Great movers in any sport are easy to spot. Watch Lleyton Hewitt racing across the court, Venus Williams ripping a backhand on the run, or Pete Sampras gliding effortlessly to the net. These athletes are not only strong and fast, but they always seem to be in balance and move effortlessly, rarely appearing awkward and seemingly always moving in the right direction. Great movers in sport are able to move effectively, efficiently, and spontaneously, flowing around the field or court without conscious thought. I believe that such movement is as much mental as it is physical—that it flows from the subconscious mind.

Dennis Van der Meer

World-renowned coach and founder and president of the Professional Tennis Registry (PTR)

I've been teaching and playing tennis for practically my entire life, but I still love to keep learning. I really strive to keep up on the latest developments in coaching. The ideas on movement and anticipation in this chapter are some of the smartest and most innovative I've come across. And that's more than mere theory! I've seen the concepts in action and can confirm how effective they truly are. I did a test with Nick where he came to net and fed me a series a balls on the baseline, and claimed he could anticipate which direction I would hit each one of my passing shots. He wouldn't necessarily hit a winner off each shot, but it was his belief that he would at least always be moving in the right direction as the ball came off my racquet. Before we started the exercise I found his assertion to be far too optimistic, but after he continually picked off each of my passing shots without hesitation, I became a firm believer.

The underlying principle to Nick's concepts is that virtually all movement should flow from the subconscious mind. In other words, moving to the ball should become an instinctual part of your tennis game. Just as with breathing or blinking, you shouldn't even have to think about it. If your opponent hits a shot and you have to think about where it's going, it's too late. You may get to the ball in time, but you're not moving at your optimal ability and your hitting options will be limited. The split-second that your eyes and brain perceive what is happening you should be racing to action. How quickly you're able to get to a ball is a huge factor in determining the quality of shot you're able to hit.

You may be saying to yourself that it's not possible to move without thinking. But if you follow the keys presented in this chapter, you'll see that it's not only possible but extremely valuable. You have to start by having the right level of intensity, yet remain relaxed enough to let your body flow. Then you have to be willing to go after each ball without regard to whether you "think" the shot will be in, out, or a winner. You have to be ready to move in any direction and then recover quickly to the correct location in order to get to the next ball. Learn to read certain cues from your opponent—ball spin and trajectory, court position, and patterns and tendencies—each of these give you a heads up on anticipating the kind of shot you'll face sometimes before it's even struck.

Whether you are a great mover or not so quick on your feet, this chapter is full of good information that will help you take your movement to a whole new level.

Secrets of Great Movement

Knowing the real secrets to great movement may not make you a great mover on the court. However, if you apply yourself and work on the principles of good movement, you will improve your court coverage more than you ever thought possible. In addition, you will be less prone to injuries and will use far less energy when you play.

Moving well in tennis is inextricably linked to virtually every aspect of the game—footwork, stroke technique, tactics, psychological state of mind, physical condition, eyesight, anticipation, and so on. All of these factors work together when you move on the tennis court. Therefore, improving your movement should not be viewed as an isolated objective or goal.

To move well in a superfast action sport such as tennis, you must have a subconscious, not conscious, thought process. What that means is that, if you are consciously thinking about how and where to move during a match, you are in big trouble. To get the process to flow from your subconscious mind, you must work on your movement skills so that they become completely automatic.

When I was a national coach, living in Princeton, New Jersey, I was asked to work with a 15-year-old girl named Lisa, who lived in nearby Pennsylvania. In particular, I was asked to help her on the forehand. I never forgot our first workout. We started hitting, and I began to analyze her forehand technique and made a few suggestions. She was clearly a very good athlete and quickly learned things. I could also see that she had the ability to move extremely well. But often, she would not run for a ball when I hit it out wide to either her forehand or backhand. So, I called her to the net and asked her a question that I already knew the answer to: "Are you a pretty fast runner?" She said, "Yes, compared to most of the girls at school." I said, "Why don't you run for the wide balls?" She replied, "I am really slow to see the ball coming off your racket." I could see that she honestly believed this, but I knew it was not the case. So, I changed the workout around and asked her to hit reflex volleys with both of us at the net. I remember being impressed with how quick she was with her hands as we fired volleys back and forth. Actually, the truth was that I was trying hard not to show that I had to be on my toes to keep up with her at the net! After a minute, I stopped the drill and said, "Lisa, do you see how quickly you pick up the ball coming off my racket during these reflex volleys? You're not even thinking about it. You just react and go. You have far less time to respond here at the net than when you are in the backcourt." She looked at me and knew I was right. I continued, "When you are in the backcourt, you can't make a conscious decision as to whether you will run or not. If you want to use that speed of yours and be a big-time player, you need to run for those wide balls first, then stop after you can't get there." The conversation took only a minute, but Lisa was very sharp and understood everything I was saying. We worked out only five or six times. However, she started moving and getting to those wide balls as she slowly began to highlight her movement skills. That was in 1989. Since that time, Lisa Raymond has developed into a top-10 singles player. But even less surprising (after our reflex volley session), she has gone on to win three Grand Slam doubles titles and has become the number-one doubles player in the world. Now when I watch Lisa on TV or at a major event hitting a great forehand on the run, my mind always flashes back to our first practice session in Princeton.

Many professional players use "movement experts" or "speed coaches" to work with them off the court to improve their movement. Although this type of training will improve your muscle strength, speed, agility, conditioning, and possibly your footwork, it only acts as a supplement to playing tennis. To master your movement skills for tennis, you must work on-court, with a racket in your hand, hitting tennis balls. There is nothing like the demands during competition, and unless you practice correctly, you'll never reach your full potential as a mover regardless of your off-court work.

I have listed what I believe are real secrets to moving up to your full potential. You could call them the "Seven Habits of Highly Effective Movers." But that would not be original, so I will just call them secrets. They are listed in sequential order. However, if you work on and improve any of these areas, your movement on the court will definitely improve. Don't try to work on all of them at once. I suggest you read this section and see if there are any areas in which you know you are weak. Then spend some time working in that area. As with most of what I talk about in this book, use this chapter as a resource that you continually come back to reinforce your understanding.

1. **Positive perception.** You must work to develop a positive perception of your ability to move. It doesn't matter if you are Michael Johnson. If you have a negative perception of your movement skills, you will not move well on the tennis court. A negative perception creates tension and self-doubt, which kill anticipation, spontaneity, and flexibility. That, in turn, produces poor movement, which reinforces the negative perception that you don't move well.

The first thing you need to do is stop any negative thoughts about your movement. Second, don't let anyone tell you that you're not a good mover or that you are slow. Third, always focus on how much you can improve. The more you can visualize yourself moving well on the court, the better. This sounds corny, but it is the foundation on which to build good movement skills. Moving well is relative to your own potential, so think positively. All players can improve and maximize their movement skills.

In 1986, I was trying to convince Michael, who at 15 years old was already one of our top juniors in the country, to represent the United States in the Sunshine Cup. This event is equivalent to the 18-and-under world team championships. The format is similar to the Davis Cup, in that the team coach (that was me) sits on the court during the match and coaches the players. The teams play two singles and one doubles, with the first team to win two matches advancing to the next round. Approximately 40 countries entered the event that year.

The problem was that Michael did not want to play because the event was played on hard tru (often called "green clay"), which is a soft surface that requires the ability to slide to the ball to be effective. Michael, whose lightning-fast speed was a cornerstone of his game, had not competed or practiced on a soft surface since the 12-and-unders. He did not feel comfortable moving and maintaining his balance on soft surfaces, and he wanted no part of playing on it. Well, it took some convincing, but he finally decided to play. So, true to his excellent work ethic, he, along with the rest of the team, practiced hard in preparation for the event. We managed to win our first two team matches to advance into the quarters. The whole team was improving with each match, but it was clear that Michael, who relied so heavily on his speed, was still not flowing in his movement. He was not fully comfortable yet on the slippery surface, which was making him consciously think about his movement, while adversely affecting his balance on the shot.

Our next match was against a tough Swedish team who were real experts on soft surfaces. We lost at the number-two singles spot (which was the first match played), so it was up to Michael to win his match to avoid giving the Swedes an insurmountable 2–0 lead in the team competition. Michael played his heart out. He moved even better than before, yet still not up to his capabilities. He simply couldn't quite match the other players' experience on the surface. Dejected, Michael sat down in the chair after losing the match and said, "I can't play on this surface. I can't use my speed on clay like I can on hard courts." I responded, "Michael, you have a perfect game for this surface. All you need is more experience so that you can move and slide without having to think about it. Believe me, you have a great game for clay." At that moment, I really don't think he believed me.

Well, I had no idea how well he would learn to play on clay. Two years later, I watched Michael Chang win the French Open on the red clay courts of Roland Garros at the age of 17. He beat the number-one player in the world, Ivan Lendl, and then Stefan Edberg in the finals in one of the biggest upset wins in professional tennis history! Needless to say, Michael had learned how to let his movement flow on the slow, red clay courts of Paris.

(continued next page)

(continued from previous page)

1986 USA Sunshine Cup Team: Jared Palmer, Jonathan Stark, Michael Chang, and Nick Saviano.

© Fred Mullane

2. **Focus on "when" not "where."** This is one of the most important keys to unleashing your movement potential. What I mean by this is that you should focus your attention on *when* your opponent is about to make contact, then start your split step right before he makes contact. Don't consciously think about where your opponent is hitting the ball. By trying not to think consciously, your subconscious thought processes take over, and you will find yourself moving in the direction of the ball as it comes off your opponent's racket. Your visual system can process information on where the ball is going infinitely quicker than you can consciously think of it. (Research shows it works as fast as 1,000th of a second in optimal conditions.) You'll also create a heightened state of awareness, both mentally and physically, enabling your brain to process incredible amounts of information when your opponent approaches the ball. It draws on previous experience and the current situation to calculate and anticipate what to expect. That is why you see the top pros instinctively flow to the ball as it comes off their opponent's racket.

I realize how complicated this sounds, but it is in fact incredibly simple. When you are competing, focus on *when* your opponent is about to contact the ball, not *where* he is going to hit it, time your split step accordingly, and you will start flowing to the ball.

3. **Be intense yet relaxed.** To move at your best, you must be in an optimum state of mental and physical preparedness. You must be intensely focused, yet physically relaxed. Don't confuse intense with tense. A tense body tightens the muscles, preventing them from reacting quickly. Watch Lleyton Hewitt during a match. He is incredibly intense, sharply concentrating on his game, yet he is so physically relaxed, it looks as if he is loafing. Then all of a sudden, he streaks across the court to reach a ball that other players cannot get. Few players will move this well, but the point has been made.

A great cue that you can use to check yourself for tenseness is to make sure your facial muscles are relaxed. If they are tense, then most likely so is the rest of your body. Also, if you are holding your breath when you hit the ball, you are holding in your tension. (You should breathe out or grunt when hitting.) Tension in the body negatively affects everything, from your vision to your footwork.

4. **Balance a book on your head.** I'm speaking figuratively, of course, but the reason is critical. As you move to the ball, maintain good upper-body posture, with your head and shoulders relatively still. In fact, you will bend forward slightly at the waist. The point is, avoid excessively bending at the waist, hunching your shoulders and/or moving your head side to side or up and down. This helps you track the ball better as it approaches. It also helps your dynamic balance, footwork, and overall technique on the shot.

5. **Maintain a low center of gravity.** As you move to the ball, keep a low center of gravity by bending your knees. See chapter 4 for a more detailed description. Show me a player who stands up straight up on the court, and I'll show you a poor mover!

6. **Run for every ball.** When the ball comes off your opponent's racket, run for it regardless of where it is going or whether you think you can get to it. The key is not to make a conscious decision initially as to whether or not to run for the ball. Just react and go for it. This will help your anticipation, your split step, your explosive first step, and your speed. You will also be able to reach balls you never dreamed of being able to get to. After at least three or four steps, if it is hopelessly out of your reach or it lands out, then you can stop running. If your opponent hits a shot and you just stand there thinking it is a winner or it is out, you have made a conscious decision. And that's a no-no.

I'll never forget the first time I was on the court with the legendary Australian coach Harry Hopman. I was 15 years old, and he had come to Northern California to do a clinic for top juniors in the area. Mr. Hopman was a fanatic when it came to effort on the practice court and running for every ball. There was a line of players waiting to spend a few minutes drilling with him. My time finally came, and Mr. Hopman started with a few relatively easy balls to get a feel for my level of play and then started firing balls all over the place. At first, I thought he accidentally hit them too far away from me, but after three or four I realized that he was serious. I stopped running for the next ball and said, "That's ridiculous. I can't get to those." Keep in mind this is the guy who had coached Rod Laver, Kenny Rosewald, Lew Hoad, John Newcombe, and Tony Roche, to name a few; and here I was, a 15-year-old kid who wasn't even nationally ranked yet. Well, everything stopped, and Harry glared at me and said, "On my court, you run for every ball or you get off the court!" He was dead serious, and I got the message. And even though at the time I did not fully understand the significance of running and stretching for every ball, I did so from then on. I can honestly say that brief lesson had a profound impact on my movement for the rest of my career. As the years went by, I worked out with Mr. Hopman countless times throughout my professional career. As he would walk out on the court with his huge basket of balls, I would joke with him and say, "Harry, you haven't got enough balls in that basket to tire me out!" He would just smile and start firing away, and I would run for every ball.

© Lance Jeffrey

Michael Chang runs and stretches for every ball.

7. **Stretch and swing.** Even if you have not quite reached the ball, stretch and swing at it and try to make the shot. First, you will surprise yourself in getting to and hitting far more balls than you ever thought possible. Second, stretching out to hit the ball helps develop your dynamic balance, footwork, and racket control.

If you apply these seven simple things, your movement will improve significantly, and you will be flowing from your subconscious mind. Keep in mind that you need to emphasize the seven keys I just talked about before moving on to more advanced techniques such as anticipation and footwork. If you skip the basic fundamentals and work only on the advanced techniques, you might not improve your movement significantly. Incorporate all the movement principles, and you'll have a winning combination.

Stages of Movement

There are four stages to your movement during a point in tennis—positioning, tracking, hitting, and recovering. You can work on all four areas at once, or you simply can focus on the stage you feel might help your particular needs. Here are the keys to success for each stage of movement.

Positioning

This is the stage when your opponent is getting ready to hit the ball. There are three crucial factors to your position. First is where you geometrically position yourself on the court in relation to where you've hit the ball. Second is the depth of your position on the court. Third is how you position your body in relation to the ball when your opponent is about to hit her shot. Note that positioning in the backcourt is different from positioning at the net. The differences will be pointed out where appropriate.

GEOMETRIC COURT POSITIONING

Geometric positioning in the backcourt is a fancy way of saying that you should recover to and/or adjust your position on the court according to where you hit your shot and where your opponent is able to hit his shot. The rule of thumb is to bisect the angle of your opponent's possible range of shots. For example, if you hit the ball to the center of the court, your position should be right in the middle of the court. If the ball is out wide to the deuce court, your position should be a few steps to the right of the centerline (see figure 5.1, page 102).

While positioning at the net is different, if you hit the volley out wide, you should position yourself a few steps closer to that sideline (see figure 5.2). Your objective is to cover the highest-percentage passing shot (which in this case is down the line) and still be able to cut off most of the crosscourt passes. That leaves your opponent with the lowest-percentage shot to hit to.

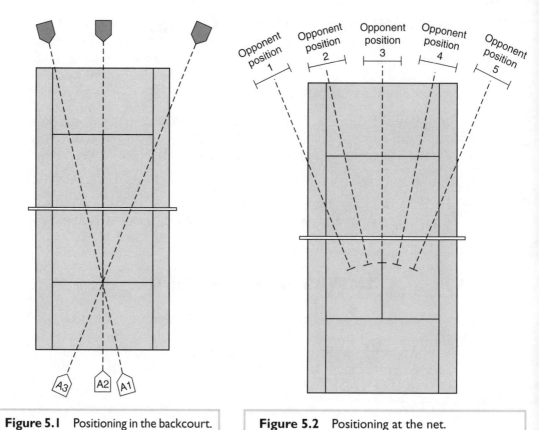

Figure 5.1 Positioning in the backcourt.

Figure 5.2 Positioning at the net.

DEPTH OF COURT

How deep you stand in the court will vary with your style of play and skill level. However, the fundamental starting position is three to five feet behind the baseline. If your opponent moves away from the net or is stretched out wide, you should move in closer to the baseline. In extreme cases, when your opponent is in a desperate position, you should step inside the baseline in anticipation of a weak, short ball or a floater you can take out of the air. If you hit a short ball and your opponent is in an aggressive position, you might want to take a step back. For positioning at the net, you should get in as close to the net as you can, while still being able to cover a lob over your head. Generally speaking, that should be about halfway between the net and the service line. However, that will vary depending on such factors as your height, your quickness, the quality of your shot, and your opponent's position on the court.

BODY POSITION

Your shoulders should be squared up to the location of the ball in your opponent's court. For example, if the ball is in the center of the court, your shoulders should be "squared up," directly toward the net. If the ball is out wide to the deuce court, your shoulders should be facing directly toward the location of the ball.

Tracking

As discussed in chapter 4, tracking involves how you move to the ball after your opponent hits his shot. Remember the keys to success. Concentrate on exploding to the ball with your first step, even if the ball is not far away from you. The faster you can get in position to hit your shot, the better. Maintain good upper body posture with minimal head movement in order to facilitate your dynamic balance.

Hitting

The hitting stage is how you set up to hit the ball. Here are two keys to execute it successfully.

1. **Adjustment steps.** As you approach the ball, take smaller steps if you have time to adjust to the ball. Your objective is to get the ball in the optimum location (distance) in relation to your body (your "hitting zone") to hit your shot.

2. **Wide base and low center of gravity.** For stability, establish a low center of gravity by having your knees bent, and keep a wide base with your feet spread at least shoulder-width apart.

Recovery

After you hit the ball, you have to move to get into position to hit the next shot. Here are three keys to successful recovery movement.

1. **A sense of urgency.** After you hit the ball, always recover with a sense of urgency. The common mistake is to take your time and watch your shot at this stage.

2. **Plant and push off.** If you are pulled out wide to either side of the court, plant your outside foot and push off, back toward the center of the court. Some players who hit with an open stance accomplish this with one movement, taking a hop/half step, in which they hit and land on the outside foot, ready to push off with that foot immediately.

3. **Face the net.** As you recover, you should face the net and take a few shuffle steps to get back into position on the court. You might use a crossover step (where one leg crosses over the other), which the pros will sometimes use to gain speed quickly to cover the necessary distance when they are pulled out wide. But if you are seriously out of position, you had better just turn and run!

In the recovery, Roger Federer plants the outside leg and begins to push off to quickly recover back into position.

Anticipation Skills

Movement skills and anticipation are inseparable. Anticipation is critical during match play because of the great demand on player movement and the minimal time available for adjustment. If you anticipate well, you will get to the ball quicker. Good anticipation skills are one of the primary reasons why the pros make the game look so easy and why they rarely seem surprised by what happens on the court. Anticipation will help you move more effectively and efficiently; you will hit the ball cleaner, be more consistent, and have fewer injuries.

Anticipation is also one of the most misunderstood terms in the game of tennis. Two misperceptions prevail. The first misperception is that anticipation can be applied only when a player knows exactly where an opponent is going to hit the ball and exactly what type of shot it will be. The second is that the only way to develop those skills is by years of experience. Though both of these thoughts are true to a certain extent, they actually represent a very small part of a much larger equation.

Anticipation can be broken down into two parts: total and partial anticipation. *Total anticipation* is when you know exactly what type of shot is coming and where it is going. How many times do you think that happens? Not very often. *Partial anticipation* is by far more common. It is the process of figuring out what your opponent cannot or will not do in a given situation. A good player does this on virtually every point.

Why is anticipation so important? Because if you can eliminate in your mind a number of options your opponent has on a given shot, it can improve your response time. (Response time is the time it takes you to react plus the time it takes you to move to the ball: reaction time + movement time = response time.) You will get to the ball much quicker, giving you more options on your shot. You also will move more freely to the ball because you will feel less stress. That freedom of movement allows you to do more with your shots. The better you anticipate, the better mover you will be.

Experience is a great teacher of anticipation. However, most players don't understand that you can train to anticipate better and cut the learning curve. It's not complicated to do. You already do this most of the time on the court, but you're simply not aware of it. By recognizing the things that will improve your anticipation, you can be more focused and directed to learn quicker. There are basically four major factors that will provide you with the information you need to anticipate on every shot.

1. **Type and quality of your opponent's shot.** By being aware of the type of shot (its direction, speed, spin, height, trajectory, and depth) and the quality of the shot, you can anticipate where and how the ball is going to bounce. Obviously, this type of anticipation occurs after your opponent has hit the ball.

2. **Patterns, tendencies, strengths, and weaknesses.** This involves knowing the patterns and tendencies of your opponent, as well as his strengths and weaknesses. Based on that information, your ability to anticipate what your opponent may or may not do improves tremendously. Scouting your opponents, practicing together, or having played them in previous matches helps you develop this type of anticipation.

3. **Opponent's court position.** This involves knowing the ramifications of your opponent's court position on the type of shot she can hit. For example, if your opponent has moved back well behind the baseline, you logically can conclude that she will not be hitting a low line drive from far behind the baseline. She most likely will hit the ball with a high net clearance to put the ball deep.

4. **Cues from opponent's stroke.** This is about your ability to pick up cues from your opponent's technique. Notice what grip he is using, his balance, the swing path of his racket, his footwork (or lack thereof), his body stance, his ball toss, and the like. All these aspects of your opponent's stroke production will give you clues as to what type of shot he is preparing to hit.

Cutting the Learning Curve

You can cut the learning curve by training specifically to improve your anticipation skills. Just by working on principles discussed so far in this chapter you naturally will improve your anticipation skills. To accelerate the learning curve even more, here are a few helpful training tips on how to specifically improve anticipation.

- **Work on pattern development.** The more familiar you are with patterns, the quicker you will recognize what your opponent's potential options are when that pattern comes up in a match. For example, if you practice the inside-out forehand pattern, in a match when you hit an inside-out forehand, you will be well aware of the potential options that your opponent might play against you, which will improve your anticipation.

- **Play games that require you to figure out your opponent's patterns and tendencies.** Tell your partner to play certain patterns and tendencies in a practice session, without telling you what they are. Then try to figure out what your partner is doing as you play points or sets. For example, your partner can choose to hit all backhands crosscourt or only attack the net behind a backhand slice down the line. Then you try to recognize the patterns and play them to your advantage.

- **Scout opponents.** The more you know about the patterns, tendencies, strengths, and weaknesses of your opponent, the better you will be at anticipating what she will do on the court.

- **Understand the effects of spin.** Slice, topspin, sidespin, and kick all affect the trajectory and bounce of the ball. Have someone hit the different types of spins to you so that you can recognize the spin and better track the ball.

- **Learn basic technique cues.** What grip does your opponent use? Where is his strike zone? Where is his toss on his serve? Does he rotate his body? Where does he stand on the return of serve? Does he hit slice? Topspin? These types of cues are essential in reading your opponent and anticipating where and how he will hit his shots. For example, if you see your opponent take the racket back well above the flight of the oncoming ball, you should anticipate a slice. If he is stretched out and reaching for the ball, look for a weak, floating reply.

- **Train consciously in practice for anticipation.** Let's say you want to get better at anticipating a passing shot. Talk with your coach about the different things to look for on the pass. If your opponent is in good position when she goes to make contact, expect a hard power shot on the pass. If she has to reach for the ball on her backhand, expect a slice, a shot down the line, or a lob.

At first, practice coming to the net and consciously thinking about what your opponent is doing. This will help assure that you know what you're looking for in order to anticipate. Then, after 10 minutes instead of thinking about where and what your opponent is doing, change your focus to *when* impact is made, take your split step, and let your thoughts flow subconsciously. The brain will naturally process the information that you have been working on.

Venus Williams is stretched out and reaching for the ball so her opponent should anticipate a weak reply from this position.

© Lance Jeffrey

Here's another example, this time on the serve. Have your partner mix up his serves while you consciously look for cues in his stroke (in other words, a toss back over his head means a kick serve, a toss to the side means a slice). After doing this for a while, shift your focus to when contact is made, start your split step right before he makes contact with the ball, and let your subconscious take over. Once your brain understands and recognizes the cues, it will automatically use this information to help you anticipate where and how he is going to serve.

Footwork

Footwork is a key fundamental of technique for every stroke in tennis. Few of us will ever possess the speed, balance, and agility of the pros, but you can, in fact, improve your court coverage by learning the fundamental techniques of good footwork and improve your overall movement skills. There are five primary objectives for footwork:

1. To get an explosive first move to the oncoming ball
2. To get to the ball quickly and efficiently while maintaining dynamic balance
3. To get your body to the optimum location in relation to the ball to execute your shot
4. To maintain good body position and static balance when appropriate (for example, on the service stance or on some ground strokes and volleys just before and/or slightly after contact)
5. To quickly recover into position after hitting the ball for the next shot

To accomplish these objectives, there are some fundamental footwork skills that every player should know. I have listed the most important techniques of footwork and what they are used for. This will help you to understand the terminology and to evaluate whether or not you are executing the footwork properly. If you have questions about any of these techniques, ask a local certified USPTA or PTR professional to help you with any of these footwork techniques.

Split Step

You should take a split step every time your opponent contacts the ball. A proper split step is arguably the most important aspect of footwork. Performing the split step at the correct time will establish your balance so that you are in a position to explode to the ball once you recognize the direction of the shot. In addition, it heightens your mental state of awareness at a critical time when the ball is coming off your opponent's racket. This helps maximize your ability to anticipate what shot is coming.

The split step is performed by bending your knees, hips, and ankles (all you need to think about is bending your knees, and your hips and ankles will bend naturally) and hopping into the air, which results in the actual *lowering* of your center of gravity as you land on the balls of your feet. The timing of the split step is crucial. You should start the split step when your opponent starts to accelerate her racket forward to hit her shot. Contrary to popular belief, your feet do not always land together on the split step. In fact, in most cases, your feet *do not* land together. What actually occurs is that you time the split step so that you are in the air when the ball comes off your opponent's racket and you are able to determine the direction the ball is being hit before you land. The result is that your foot farthest from the ball lands first, while your foot closest to the ball actually turns to point in the direction of the shot before it lands. This enables you to make an explosive first step to the ball. Most players do this stepping-out action naturally and are unaware that they make this move. I suggest that you *not* work on this stepping-out action—leave it to instinct. Rather, I would suggest focusing on the timing of your split step.

(a) Mark Philippoussis takes a small hop as he executes a split step. *(b)* Note how his right foot lands first and the left foot turns in the direction in which he is going to move before it lands.

© Lance Jeffrey

Keys to Learning the Split Step

- *Good posture.* Maintain good posture in your upper body, keeping your shoulders and back relatively straight with your waist bent slightly forward.
- *Squaring up to your opponent.* You do not want to be turned at an angle when your opponent contacts the ball. You need to be facing directly toward your opponent. This will help ensure that you are balanced and ready to explode in any direction.
- *Timing.* Start your split step right before your opponent contacts the ball, preferably when she starts the forward motion of her racket.
- *Height of the jump.* Don't take a high jump. You should hop or jump just a few inches off the ground, with the intent of lowering your center of gravity and landing on the balls of your feet, which should be at least shoulder-width apart, with knees, hips, and ankles bent.

Changing Direction

To stop as quickly as possible and recover, plant your outside leg, bend your knees, and get your weight leaning in the direction you want to move. Your inside foot should be pointed in the direction in which you are recovering. Then push off and explode back in the opposite direction. It is critical not to let your inertia push you off balance, which will force you to take extra steps to recover. Quick changes of direction require excellent leg strength.

Shuffle Step

When there's only a short distance to get to the ball or to recover position, most players use a shuffle step. You cannot cover as much ground with the shuffle step, but it is easier and quicker to establish your balance, as opposed to using a crossover step. In the shuffle step, face the net and push off with your outside leg toward the direction you want to go. Your inside leg starts to push off before your outside leg lands, with both of your feet meeting in midair right before your outside foot lands. A common mistake is to use the shuffle step to cover a large distance when it would be more effective to use the crossover.

Crossover Step

When you are pulled out wide of the court and need to recover quickly, use the crossover step. In most cases, plant your outside leg and push off to start the recovery. Then cross your outside leg over in front of your inside leg, with your upper body facing the net. The crossover step enables you to

Marat Safin displays beautiful form—good upper body posture and dynamic balance—as he executes the crossover step.

cover as much ground as possible with your first step without committing to one side of the court or the other.

Two-Step Recovery

A two-step recovery is executed when you are forced out wide on a dead run and need to stop your momentum and recover. Contact the ball off your back foot, and after your front foot lands, your back foot crosses behind and plants to change direction. Because your momentum has pulled you far off the court and this recovery takes longer to execute, you should usually try to hit a neutralizing or defensive shot that will give you time to recover or try to hit a winner.

Hop/Half-Step Recovery

This maneuver is used when you are pulled out wide but not on a dead run and want to stop as quickly as possible and change directions after hitting the ball. Hit the ball with an open stance and take a small recovery step with your outside leg (it actually looks like a hop). Then, planting your outside foot, bend at your knees, and, with your weight leaning back toward the center of the court, push off to recover. This saves about a half step in recovery time. Because more and more players are using an open stance on both the backhand and forehand, this type of footwork is extremely common.

Jennifer Capriati executes the hop/half-step for a quick recovery.

a

b

Drop Step

The drop step is your first step back to cover a lob. Right-handers should step back with their right foot first. As you take this first step back, your upper body starts to turn to facilitate a quick move back for the overhead.

Movement Killers

The most common mistakes you can make that will "kill" your movement skills and limit you from reaching your full potential. Talk with a certified USPTA or PTR coach, or ask a friend to watch you play to see if any of these movement killers apply to you.

- Excessive dead-ball drills, instead of live-ball drills or playing points and competition. There are many excellent dead-ball drills, that can enhance your movement, but they should not take the place of live-ball drills.
- Excessive drilling where you know where the ball is going to be hit
- Improper drilling where the ball is aimlessly fed to the player
- Negative talk or thoughts about your movement skills
- Consciously thinking about where the ball is going
- Not running after every ball
- Not reaching and swinging for balls out of your reach
- Poor posture, such as excessively bending over at your waist, hunching your shoulders, or a lot of head movement when running
- Poor conditioning
- Poor coordination skills
- Improper footwork, particularly on the split step

Before you go and decide what aspects of your movement you need to work on, once again I suggest you review and apply the seven points I addressed at the beginning of the chapter. If you faithfully implement them you will naturally start to apply many of the movements and specific footwork. Just don't try to do too much at once. Also, talk with your teaching pro if you have questions. But remember, having the feeling that you are flowing around the court and maximizing your movement skills will not only improve your game but it is also a real joy.

Simulate for Success

> Re-create match conditions in practice to prepare for every physical and mental challenge your opponents can throw at you.

At all levels of play—including the professional ranks—players often do as much damage to their games during practice as they gain in benefit. Or, I could say, they often "unlearn" more during practice sessions than they learn. Sad but true! How can that happen? Easy. Mindless hitting, poor practice habits, and ineffective and counterproductive drills make players ill-prepared for the demands they face in competition. Practice makes perfect? Not in this context. Hard work pays off? Not necessarily, if you work hard at the wrong things. The truth is closer to the dictum, "Practice like you play, and play like you practice." Optimum practice will create optimum results.

Brad Gilbert

Formerly ranked top 5 in the world and coach of Andre Agassi

Want to become a better tennis player? Want to win more matches? The answer is simple—practice. But the catch is you've got to practice the right way. I'm a really big proponent of quality practice. Practice is where it all happens. In my opinion, practicing is more important than any other aspect of a player's development. If you're not performing well in practice, your game isn't going to magically take off in a match.

That's why it's so important to give your practice structure and try to simulate what happens in a match. It's not about going out there for hours and aimlessly bashing the ball around. That's overkill: You'll fry your brain and end up actually hurting your game. You can spend less than half the time out there, and if you're constructive and focused you can make great improvements. Tennis is like a book that never ends. You have to constantly keep writing new chapters by working to stay ahead of the game. Even a player as accomplished as Andre Agassi would always approach his practice with a purpose and a direction. He's getting better with age because he's constantly thinking that what he has isn't good enough and could be even better. Whether it's a subtle change in his grip or adjusting his technique on the volley, Andre is always thinking about something he can improve.

That's why I like this chapter—Nick goes over some of the most important points for how to practice the right way. All you need to do is pay attention. You'll understand the benefit of having clear objectives for your practice and incorporating key mental aspects into each session. You'll see the difference between learning a new stroke and building your game to get more confident each day leading up to a big match. You'll learn to touch on all aspects of your game and simulate the same situations you would during competition. It doesn't make any sense to practice things that aren't going to happen when you're playing for real, and you don't want to become a player that can only perform when it doesn't matter. If you simulate match conditions in practices and you're able to execute well under those circumstances that's a good indication that when it's time to play, you're going to bring your best. That's what taking practice seriously is all about.

Making the Most of Your Time

If you want to make the most of your practice time, simulate the demands you face in competition—technically, tactically, emotionally, intellectually, and physically. This not only keeps your practices challenging and stimulating, but it also prepares you for the challenges you'll face during match play and creates a positive learning process that will catapult you to the next level.

Within this context you should take into consideration your game style and strategy and structure your practices to improve and add to your game. Your developmental plan will make it clear to you what areas are most important for you to emphasize.

When I played on the pro tour, I occasionally trained at a popular tennis facility. The place had a great atmosphere, good players, good coaches, and everyone there worked very hard. I would train there for a week at a time, practicing up to five hours a day. I got in great physical condition and felt I was hitting the ball well. However, every time I left to compete in a tournament, I felt slow moving to the ball and played terribly. At first I thought it was a coincidence, but after it happened four or five times, I realized the problem was related to how I was practicing.

What I figured out was that most of the drilling I was doing at the facility did not simulate what would happen in a match. In fact, I was inadvertently unlearning things about movement and tactics that previously had come naturally. For example, in one drill, the coach would stand on the baseline in the deuce court, and I would be at the net. The coach would fire five balls in a row at me, moving me all over the net, and occasionally throw up a lob. This drill felt great; I had to move a lot, hit a lot of balls, and got a great physical workout. The problem was that there is little correlation between the patterns in this drill—the decision making, shot selection, and movement—and what occurs in a match. Say the coach fires a ball down the line, and I hit the volley crosscourt. In a match, I would then quickly recover and move to the other side of the court, getting in position according to where my shot landed. But, instead, the next ball in this drill would come from the coach, who was still standing in the deuce court. The result was I was unlearning the proper recovery moves and didn't learn to position myself correctly. I used to do this drill 30 minutes at a time, six days a week. It's no wonder I felt slow and out of sync during matches. This is just one simple example. Eventually I learned that I had to be much more cognizant of the way I practiced, not just practicing hard.

To help you simulate for success, there are some specific objectives that you need to know to make sure you are maximizing your practice sessions, as well as some of the most common mistakes that are made during training.

Know Your Objectives

If you don't know what you are trying to accomplish, chances are you will not accomplish much. It is important to have specific objectives when you go out to practice. Obviously, your objectives will change depending on a number of factors, such as how much time before your next competition, how important the competition is, what surface you will be playing on, and the like. In addition, you must be clear about what specifically you are working on. Is it technique or tactics or both? Are you trying to develop a weapon or improve a weakness? There are so many variables regarding your practice objectives that I cannot possibly cover every possibility. Instead, by providing some key principles of high-quality practice, I will provide you with the tools to accomplish your own practice objectives, whatever they may be.

• **Quality.** If you want to play high-quality tennis, you want to have high-quality practice sessions. This sounds trite, but it is true. As Aristotle stated, "We are what we repeatedly do. Excellence is therefore not an act, but a habit."

• **Purposeful training.** As I just said, your practice sessions should have a purpose. You can grow in skill, knowledge, and enjoyment during the session if you are aware of what you are doing and why. You don't want to engage in mindless training where you put little thought into it, don't understand much, and don't learn anything new. Have some kind of plan, even if it is as simple as playing points and working on good shot selection. Note the errors you make and how to correct them. Conversely, be aware of the good things you do during the session and how you executed them. With this approach, you will grow in appreciation of the practice session. Remember, two shots in tennis are never exactly alike, which means the learning process never stops. So, when you are practicing, always think about what you are doing, how to improve it, and what you are trying to accomplish.

• **Whole versus part.** A theory states that the whole equals more than the sum of its parts. Change any one part and the whole system is changed. In terms of tennis, that means it is better to learn the whole stroke or the technique and the tactics that apply to it at once, as opposed to learning it in parts. Let me explain. Let's say you are learning to hit a forehand, and you learn each phase of the stroke separately—first the footwork, then the backswing, then the hitting action, and finally the follow-through. You have technically learned all the parts of the entire stroke. However, this method is not the same or as effective as learning the whole stroke at once. The point here is that, when you break down a stroke into parts and then rebuild it, it is not as effective as learning the whole stroke at once. This is also true with regards to separating technique and tactics. Avoid learning technique by itself, as I discussed earlier in chapter 4 on technique. Always try to learn the entire skill at once if you can. If you need to break down the stroke to learn it, that is fine. But make sure you try to incorporate the whole process as soon as possible.

• **Dynamic versus static movement.** Tennis is a game of movement. So, don't try to learn strokes in a static position. This follows up on what I just said about the "whole versus part" theory. Part of the whole process of the stroke is the movement to and from the ball. Therefore, try to incorporate movement, which includes acceleration to the ball and deceleration to hit and recover, into any learning process so as to better simulate match play. This will help transfer the skill from practice to competition.

• **Learn correctly first.** Pay now or pay a lot more later! Once you learn something incorrectly, it is far more difficult to unlearn the error and then learn the proper technique—like biting your nails. So, remember, this is not just for *your* game but also for your child if he or she is playing the game. Once players learn something the incorrect way, it is extremely difficult to correct later on. Always try to learn the technique correctly the first time and save yourself a great deal of time and frustration later on.

Mental Aspects of a Good Practice

A good practice session requires key mental aspects. You may only use a few at a time, but you should constantly be looking to incorporate these aspects into your practice sessions.

1. **Concentration.** Focus on what you are doing and have a purpose to what you are doing. Mindless hitting will not help your game.

2. **Court awareness.** Develop good perception skills. Always be aware of where you are on the court and tactically how that should affect your shot selection. In other words, when you are practicing, always try to hit the correct shot, given the situation. Often players get lazy during practice and hit shots they otherwise would not hit in a match and then rationalize that it's okay because they wouldn't do that in a match. Be assured, though, it will come back to haunt you.

It was the final day of the French Junior championships in Paris. Jared Palmer— one of the most talented and creative shot makers I have had the opportunity to work with—was battling a French junior, named Fabrice Santoro, in front of thousands of chanting French fans. Throughout that European tour, I had warned and pleaded with Jared not to consistently hit in practice this trick forehand volley, where he would create a tremendous angle off of a standard shot. I said, "Jared, if you keep hitting that shot in practice, it will come back to haunt you in a match." It was 6–5 in the third set, match point for Jared, an incredibly tense situation. Jared attacked the net, and Santoro came up with an unbelievable passing shot on the line—and I mean on the line—to bring it back to deuce. The crowd was going crazy. Jared attacked the net again and Santaro hit a weak reply. All Jared had to do was hit a standard forehand volley to the open court, and he would have had another match point. But for just a split second, Jared started to hit the trick forehand volley, then quickly attempted to convert to his normal shot. But it was too late. He missed the volley in the tape! It may or may not have cost him the match but nevertheless, he unfortunately lost 8-6 in the third. So, believe me when I say how and what you do in practice will come out in matches!

3. **Anticipation.** You will naturally learn to anticipate by doing proper live-ball drilling and playing points and games. And you can also do specific types of practice that will enhance anticipation. But always be aware of drills, particularly excessive dead-ball drilling, that can damage anticipation.

4. **Decision making.** Incorporate drills into your practices that require you to make decisions regarding what type of shot to make and where to hit it, as opposed to always knowing in advance where you will hit the ball. For example, if you are doing a basic crosscourt backhand-to-backhand drill from the backcourt, try changing to a drill in which you go backhand to backhand until you get a short ball, and then hit it down the line. This requires that you recognize the short ball and make a decision to hit a different shot. That simple change creates a better learning experience.

5. **Problem solving.** Address specific problems and situations on the court, such as how to exploit a weakness, playing someone with a big forehand, and so on.

6. **Tactical understanding.** Instead of mindless repetition of the same shots, work on shot selection, how to counter an opponent, how to develop patterns, and how to get the shot you want.

7. **Self-evaluation.** Look in the mirror and evaluate your own play, whether it be technique, tactics, or the psychological aspects of your game. Don't just rely on your coach telling you what to do. The more aware you are of what is going on, the better you will be at tactically adjusting.

Learning Versus Performance

As I stated in chapter 5 on movement, you want to put yourself in the optimum state physically and mentally during your practices. This optimum state is intense yet relaxed. When appropriate, you should learn to practice at the same pace and intensity that you would use playing a match. There are times when you will need to slow things down, such as when learning a new stroke, experimenting with technique, or trying some new creative tactics. But for the most part, you should be in the optimum state when you practice.

Though you should always be learning when you step on the court, generally speaking you have two major modes of execution: the *learning mode* and the *performance mode*. The learning mode is when you are learning a new skill or working on improving an existing one, which requires considerable conscious thought. The performance mode is when your main focus is on performing in competition or to gauge the level of skill you have acquired.

It is important to know which state you are in and practice accordingly. For example, if you are trying to work on the technique for your new backhand slice, it is not the time to go out and play a highly competitive match. It is fine to play a practice match while in a learning mode, with the understanding that you are working on the new technique. The key point is to know what mode you are working in and then set up your practices accordingly.

Drilling and Training—Live Versus Dead Ball

Better to be "live than dead!" Tennis drills are typically classified either as live-ball or dead-ball drills. Both types of drills have their merits. If you want a drill that replicates the demands of a real match situation, a live-ball drill will be best. On the other hand, if you are really struggling with the technical aspects of a stroke and want a lot of repetition or you are introducing a new pattern of play, a dead-ball drill may be more appropriate. On the whole, live-ball drills are preferable to dead-ball drills because they simulate real play more closely.

DEAD-BALL DRILLS

A dead-ball drill consists of repetitive ball feeds from another player or coach. The drill is initiated from a "dead" ball, wherein the coach feeds the ball to the player from a standing location either on or next to the court. Dead-ball drills can be used for various reasons, such as movement, pattern, and tactical training, but most often they are used to learn or improve technique.

The major benefit of dead-ball drilling is that the player receives a consistent ball to hit regardless of where her previous shot goes. You can get a lot of repetitions for a particular stroke or pattern of shots. You can design dead-ball drills to closely simulate match play by manipulating the type, speed, and location of the feed. You also can expand the benefit of the drill by using specific patterns and targets. The disadvantage of a dead-ball drill is that the drill does not simulate the back-and-forth hitting that happens when you are playing a point and thus does not by itself adequately prepare you for competition. It also inadvertently can diminish anticipation skills of reading cues from opponents' strokes and positioning.

LIVE-BALL DRILLS

A live-ball drill consists of rallies between you and another player or coach. Live-ball drills can provide you with opportunities to work on many skills, including anticipation, conditioning, decision-making skills, pattern development, footwork, and stroke mechanics. Within the context of these drills, you can either create a drill that simulates match play or narrow the focus of the drill to develop one particular skill.

The advantage of a live-ball drill over a dead-ball drill is that a good live-ball drill naturally simulates actual game situations with variations such as different speeds, spins, locations, height of the ball, and so on. These types of drills more closely simulate what happens in match play, providing greater carryover from practice to play. The frustrating thing about live-ball drilling is that you will probably make more errors than with dead-ball drills because of the increased difficulty of the rallies.

Simulation Enhancers: Things to Incorporate

- Vary the spin, speed, and location of the ball fed to you in drills.
- When drilling, create uncertainty as to where the ball is going.
- Incorporate live-ball drilling frequently.
- Practice at your optimum state, physically and mentally.
- Practice at or above the speed or greater than you will play in a match.
- Play with different types of players.
- Give yourself the proper amount of rest between rallies while drilling.
- Create pressure in your practices.
- Hit each ball with a purpose.
- Practice open-ended drilling to incorporate decision making and shot selection.
- Practice the patterns that play into your strengths.

Work-to-Rest Ratio

Take time to rest! You can only run hard for so long before your technique and concentration start to break down and the overall benefit of the work-out starts to diminish. When you are running hard in practice, think in terms of work-to-rest ratio, such as 1 to 1, 1 to 2, or 1 to 3. This is a fancy way of saying that, if you run hard for 10 seconds (which is longer than almost any point you will ever play in a match), take at least 10 seconds to rest (1 to 1) or 20 seconds (1 to 2). If you are doing a lot of repetitions, you will often need 30 seconds (1 to 3) to recover. After doing this five to seven times, you will probably need to sit down and take 60 to 90 seconds' rest, just as you would during a changeover during a match. It may not sound very strenuous, but even top world-class professionals would be exhausted within 45 minutes if they tried to practice without a proper work-to-rest ratio. Granted, if you practice only by standing in one place and hitting balls, you are not really exerting yourself; but that type of training should be avoided if at all possible. I have seen more eager tennis players and potentially good practice sessions destroyed by a lack of understanding of this one simple concept.

That is not to say that you should never push yourself to the point of fatigue when practicing—quite to the contrary. However, if you do, make every effort to maintain the quality of your stroke. The intensity of your practice, how much you are running, your conditioning level, and your age will all affect how much and how often you will need to rest. But remember that proper rest is an important part of a successful practice.

Time per Training Session

The length of a practice session will vary significantly depending on such factors as your objectives, age, weather, and the like. Most pros, however, will not exceed two hours for a training session. More is not necessarily better. For the average adult, 90 minutes is plenty. Even top juniors should not exceed two hours at a time. Obviously, well-conditioned athletes can practice twice a day if they are serious about improving their game. However, the key point is quality versus quantity.

Many years ago, before the start of the Australian Indoor championships, a young Eliot Telscher (he reached top five in the world rankings a few years later) and I got up early two days in a row to practice with Jimmy Connors at the stadium court. It was actually the only court they had, and all of the matches were being played there. So we had to book the court early, in this case 7:00–8:00 A.M., simply to get the court for an hour. When you practiced with Jimmy, you didn't want to be late, so Eliot and I got there at 6:45 A.M. Jimmy was already there jogging around the baseline, then doing some jump rope. We then started to warm up, with Eliot and I on one side and Jimmy on the other. Oh, boy, you had to be ready because Jimmy would start right out moving his feet quickly, getting in perfect position for every ball. And even though we were not hitting hard yet, it was already a workout—Jimmy got to the ball early so that you had less time than normal to get to the ball, and he would rarely miss. Needless to say, we warmed up quickly. Then we would warm up our serves and play points. Eliot and I would alternate playing points against Jimmy. It was an amazing experience! Jimmy ran for every ball and made us work for every point. His intensity and commitment to quality were real eye-openers to both of us, let alone fatiguing. Toward the end of the session after Eliot had just finished playing a long point, I said, "Have you ever gotten this tired in a one-hour practice?" He just looked at me, shook his head, and said, "Are you kidding? I'm exhausted!" In those two days, we both learned a great deal about the quality of practice and that you don't have to hit for hours at a time to get a great workout. By the way, it was not a coincidence that I had a good tournament and reached the semifinals before losing to, you guessed it, Jimmy Connors.

Jimmy Connors practiced with the same intensity he brought to the competition.

© Associated Press

Accuracy Versus Power

More power equals less accuracy. Players want to emulate the pros and incorrectly believe that they should blast every ball as hard as they can. This just isn't the case. Professionals use spin and variations of speed to control the ball. Another misperception is that the pros always hit for the lines. Actually, in most cases, they have larger target areas than you think.

A lot of people rip the cover off the ball and miss most of their shots, thinking that someday their shots will start to go in. But missing every other ball in practice is not going to do you any good (not to mention that no one will want to hit with you!). I suggest that you use the 50 percent rule. Set your target areas so that you can hit them 50 percent of the time. If you can hit them more often than that, set smaller target areas. For example, if you are a beginner, your targets should be just to get the ball over the net and in the court. As your skill improves, your target can become one-half of the court. A more advanced player may set his target areas at five to seven feet in diameter. World-class pros might have target areas as small as two feet wide. On the serve, pros will aim within inches of where they intend to serve. You may want to start by hitting the serve in a general direction first, before shrinking your targets.

The point is power can be good, but you have to realize that more power equals less accuracy. If you are hitting the ball hard, set bigger target areas. If you are making too many mistakes, either slow down the pace of your shots or aim for a larger target area.

Patterns of Play

Working on developing patterns of play that you will use in a match is one of the best ways to simulate match play in practice. I would recommend that, in addition to practicing patterns simply to improve a specific skill, try to perfect patterns that play into your strengths and that force players away from your weaknesses.

For example, if you have a good backhand and a weak forehand you might want to work on the crosscourt backhand pattern than rip the ball down the line when you get the short ball so that you can highlight your backhand more frequently. And practice a forehand down the line off of your opponent's crosscourt backhand pattern. This will force your opponent to hit the next shot to your backhand. Refer to chapter 3, where I give details regarding which patterns are most important for your particular game style.

Closed-Ended Versus Open-Ended Drilling

When you are trying to improve the patterns and shot selections you make in a match, use what is called open-ended drills, as opposed to closed-ended drills. A closed-ended drill is when you know exactly what shots you will hit during the drill. Let's say you are practicing the inside-out

World-Class Practice Session

Here is an example of a recent practice session I had with Jan-Michael Gambill (U.S. Davis Cup player and top 20 in the world) and his father/coach, Chuck. From reading this, you can see how some of the basic principles in this chapter are applied. You can also use this session as a guide to set up your own practice.

- Primary objective of session: Work on the return of serve, with emphasis on the forehand return

- Goal: More consistency and improved movement to the ball

- Warm-up: Went through standard warm-up, stretching and hitting all of his shots. Made sure he broke a sweat.

- Targets for return: Set up large target areas away from the lines for high-percentage returns. Used tennis balls to "outline" target area.

- Ten minutes of returns without playing the point: In this segment, the objectives were to execute the high-percentage return to the large areas and monitor the fundamentals of technique on the return. His partner served mostly to his forehand but occasionally to his backhand, to ensure that preparation for the return simulated match play. If Jan-Michael knows that the ball is only going to his forehand, he has a tendency to turn before the hit, or "cheat" to the forehand side, which does not simulate match play.

- Play out the points: After feeling comfortable with the mechanics and the locations of the returns, he moved on to playing regular points. He did this for another 10 to 15 minutes but didn't keep score. At this stage, we didn't want him to be too competitive. We continued to monitor technique and shot selection.

- Competitive point play: The next stage was to play 30 minutes of competitive points, with both players alternating between serving and returning.

- Finish with tiebreaker: We finished the session with a highly competitive tiebreaker for a soft drink. This provides a good measure of how he is now executing the return.

- Recap of session: We discussed what worked, how the return felt, and any suggestions for future workouts.

Jan-Michael Gambill quickly learned the importance of simulating match conditions in practice and used that time to improve on his weaknesses.

© Lance Jeffrey

forehand. The drill you set up calls for you to hit the ball inside out to your partner's backhand. Your partner hits or feeds the reply down the line, and you run over and hit your forehand crosscourt. This is a perfectly good way to practice the pattern, but there is basically no decision making involved.

To take the drill to a higher level and more closely simulate match play, add variation and decision making to turn the drill into an open-ended drill. For example, using this same drill, hit the ball inside out, and let your partner have the option of hitting or feeding the next ball either down the line or crosscourt. That forces you to make the proper shot selection and hit the right shot. You are practicing the same pattern (the inside-out forehand) but also learning the different options and shot-selection decisions.

Weapon Development

Don't let your weapons rust. Andre Agassi has one of the best forehands of all time, but I always see him practice the shot. Pete Sampras consistently practices his serve. Lindsay Davenport never fails to practice her ground strokes. The point is that all the great players never neglect their weapons. Practice your weapons, and work on pattern developments that play into your strengths.

Adversity Training

"I always choke under pressure!" How many of you have said that to yourself? How about, "If I could only play in matches the way I play in practice, I would be happy." Boy, do I know that feeling!

There are many reasons for the discrepancy between practices and match play, but one of the best ways to bridge that gap is through adversity training. I first heard this term used by Dan Gould PhD, a sport psychologist, who has worked a great deal with U.S. Olympic athletes, and I have used it ever since. The idea is to train in an environment that produces some of the adversity and pressure you face in a match. If it is windy outside, don't skip practice or play indoors. Get out there and play. How else are you going to learn to deal with the wind in a match other than to practice in windy conditions? What about facing a player who hits with too much topspin or too much power? Learn to deal with it in practice, and you will handle it better in a match. One big area that people need to deal with is pressure. Try to simulate pressure in your practices. Challenge yourself in drills by seeing how many shots you can make, or keep score in a drill or practice set and play for soft drinks. To simulate an audience, ask a friend or two to watch you play a set. Play a practice match against someone whom you know you should beat. Learn to deal with adversity in practice so that you are better prepared to deal with it in a match.

Remember, if you want to optimize your time on the court, simulate the demands of competition in your practice. By doing this, you will be amazed at how much your game will improve over a short time. For more specifics on what particular drills you should use or how to set up your personal practice sessions, contact a local certified USPTA or PTR professional to help you out. Practice like you play and play like you practice, and you will get the maximum results you want.

Focus On What You Can Control

> "Everyone faces mental challenges on the court. The key to overcoming them is to zero in on what is within your ability and ignore the rest."

I am not a sport psychologist, but as a coach, I play one on the tennis court every day. After 35 years of playing, coaching, and observing tennis at all levels of the game and interacting with some of the top sport psychologists, I have been able to formulate what I believe are rock-solid principles of sport psychology. They are concepts that are used by the top professionals in the world. Are they secrets? No and yes. They are not secrets in that many knowledgeable people are aware of them; however, they are secrets in that so few players understand their significance or apply them. One thing is for sure. If you see a great champion competing, she is using many or all of these secrets. They are simple concepts, straightforward and easy to grasp. Yet, they actually transcend all sports and can maximize your ability to perform in competition in all walks of life. If you work on and improve any of the following areas, it will have a significant impact on your game.

Dick Gould

Men's tennis coach Stanford University, and coach of 17 NCAA Championship teams

Here's the simple truth: You can play the best tennis of your life and still lose a match. You can even play some of your worst tennis and still find a way to win. Why? Because in tennis the end result can often be out of our control. Some days our best just isn't good enough. It is the ability to focus on what you can control and executing to the best of your ability under the circumstances that makes someone a great competitor. In other words, your mental game is critical to your success as a player.

There are so many factors in a match completely out of your control that can wreak havoc on your psyche. For instance, say you're involved in a back and forth match and on a big point your opponent's forehand hits the net chord and just dribbles over on your side. Or you play a great point and set up an easy overhead that the wind all of a sudden decides to blow back to the baseline and out of your reach. Sound familiar? The only way to prevent these nightmare situations from damaging your overall performance is by being mentally fit. That is why this chapter on the psychology of tennis is so important.

Being the best you can be *mentally* rarely comes naturally. People often say it takes experience to learn to win. But I think that can be a rather a nebulous term. Playing a lot of matches that don't challenge you won't help you when the score finally gets close. What you need is the right kind of experience. Being put in pressure situations in tournament matches and in practice helps you to learn to focus on what can be controlled—helping you build a winning attitude learning to focus on what can be controlled is what makes a winning attitude. It's not easy. You have to take the time to exercise your mind as well as your body.

Being a college coach, I get to play the role of psychologist to my players during the course of the match. What I've found over my many years of coaching is that when a player is struggling, their concentration wanders from the job at hand. It's my responsibility to ask them questions about their strategy in order to force them to refocus on each point and get them competing better. Nick provides the techniques to do this exact exercise in this chapter. He presents 13 tips that serve as a cornerstone to developing a solid mental approach to the game. They are real and essential fundamentals that will help players at all ability levels play and compete at their very best. Even if you have all the physical tools in the world, you won't be a great player unless you have the mental game to match.

Psychological Secrets of the Champions

From a psychological perspective, your goal when you are competing is to put yourself into the optimum psychological state of mind. That will almost automatically put you into the optimum physical state because the two are inextricably linked. Sport psychologists often call this the ideal performance state. You may know it as being "in the zone." This is a state of intense focus and concentration, while being relaxed. An athlete performs at his absolute best in this state. We've all seen great athletes who are in the zone. It's a beautiful thing to watch.

Getting into this state does not happen often for any athlete at any level. Therefore, I don't want to make this the primary focus of this chapter. Rather, I will discuss the key concepts that you need to understand so that you can strive to achieve or get closer to your ideal performance state as frequently as possible. Doing this will consistently elevate your level of play, and you'll derive a greater enjoyment from the game.

The following concepts are the psychological principles that are used by the champions. They are in sequential order of priority and inextricably linked. Doing the first one will help you achieve the next and so on.

Secret 1

⬤ *Focus on only those things that you can control and disregard the rest* ⬤

This is the first and most important concept, and it must be the foundation from which to build your psychological approach to competition. If you can grasp and apply it, it will help to free you psychologically and physically to play the best tennis you are capable of.

Great athletes mention this concept all the time. Sometimes, they say it in fewer words, yet we often don't seem to hear them. Monica Seles (who I felt was one of the greatest competitors I had ever seen in any sport before her unfortunate attack by a crazed fan) said before the 2000 French Open: "I truly will try to worry about things I can control and not worry about stuff that's really outside of my control." Andre Agassi was quoted by *USA Today* before a tournament as saying: "If I come in here physically ready and hungry, then I'm giving myself the best shot to win here." And perhaps John Wooden, the great basketball coach at UCLA, said it best: "The more concerned we become over the things we can't control, the less we will do with the things we can control."

Why is this so important? If you are not focusing on what you can control, you are no longer giving yourself the best chance to play up to your potential. It will create problems such as fear, anxiety, frustration, significant fluctuations in motivation, and stagnation in your development. It will also affect your ability to analyze the match and to adjust tactically.

Gustavo Kuerten has an excellent competitive approach—intense, yet relaxed. It is not unusual to see him smile on the court!

Conversely, when you are engrossed in what you can control, you will find that you are more relaxed and your concentration improves. The result is that you not only strike the ball better but your ability to analyze the match and make good tactical adjustments is enhanced. Finally, and most important, you will enjoy the competition! Don't get me wrong. You should be aware of such things as your opponent, the score, the environment, and the like, but they are simply a means to gather information so that you know what actions you might take. The most difficult aspect of this concept for players to buy into is that they can't control winning and losing. The phrase "I control my own destiny" is not totally true on a tennis court or in life. Here are a few examples that may help illustrate this point.

Imagine that you are playing Andre Agassi in a two-out-of-three-point contest. Can he guarantee winning the points? No. He might make an unforced error or twist his ankle, or you might hit a let cord that drops for a winner. Even against you, Andre cannot control winning and losing. What he can control, however, is how he plays, the pace between points, his shot selection, and so on. If he focuses on the things he can control (which he does to a great extent), your odds of beating him won't be good!

It doesn't matter what the situation may be. You don't control winning and losing. You can profoundly affect the outcome and put the odds in your favor by focusing on what you can control. Positively affect what you can, and don't worry about what you can't. You'll be surprised at how successful you'll become. Once you let go of the false notion that you can completely determine the outcome, you'll find that you are more likely to get the outcome you want.

When you catch your mind drifting toward the mental quicksand of things you cannot control (which means no chance for a "flow state"), tell yourself to stop and refocus. Get yourself back on solid ground by focusing on the things you can affect. When you are able to do this, you are a major step closer to achieving your optimum state, physically and mentally. Your chances of being able to flow in your play and reaching your ideal performance state are far better. The remaining secrets are all things that you have a great deal of control over and are inextricably tied to the first secret.

Things You Cannot Control

- Winning and losing. (It doesn't matter whether it's the point, the game, or the match. You can affect the outcome, but you cannot control it.)
- How your opponent plays on a given point, in a game (or the match)
- The environment, such as wind, sun, rain, and so on (Remember that you can control how you deal with them, and that's a big difference!)
- Unfortunate breaks, such as let cords, mis-hits, bad bounces, and so on
- How someone else is doing in a tournament or the rankings
- What other people are going to think about your game or your results

Secret 2

● *Winning is not the number-one goal when you are competing* ●

Winning is extremely important, and, of course, it is always one of your most important goals for competition. But when winning becomes your number-one goal during competition, it will psychologically consume you because you will be focusing your energies on something you cannot control. This will distract you from executing your game to the best of your ability. At that point, you are no longer giving yourself the best chance to win, and that means you are not going to win as often. Great champions know this concept well, and the bigger the match, the more they attempt to discipline their mind. Concentrating on the things they can control, they know that winning will be a by-product of executing to the best of their ability.

Winning, as your number-one goal, in reality means striving for mediocrity relative to what you are capable of. The question is not whether you win or lose. Billie Jean King said: "When you stay in the process is when you win. Not when you get into the end results." The question is did you do everything in your power to give yourself the best chance to play up to your potential and are you constantly trying to improve? After Tiger Woods won his third Masters championship, everyone was speculating on how many majors he would win. What he said illustrates my point: "The thing I keep saying to myself is that I want to become a better player at the end of the year. And if I can keep doing that year after year for the rest of my career, I'll have a pretty good career." That is the pursuit of personal excellence! Winning is a natural by-product of this pursuit. The commitment to personal excellence does not guarantee winning. It does, however, ensure success. The end result is that you will win far more than you otherwise would have, and you will often exceed your self-imposed limitations.

Rising American star Andy Roddick, as he was preparing for the 2001 French Open, said, "I really don't have any expectations [concerning winning or losing]. I want to play well [in other words, execute his game]. If someone is going to beat me, I want him to have to play a good match [concentrating only on what he can control]."

Later in the year, as Roddick was preparing for the 2001 U.S. Open after winning four tour events, he said, "I'm just going to go in and try to play well [focus on what he can control], have some fun, and see what happens." Andy reached the quarterfinals, where he lost 6–4 in the fifth set to the eventual champion Lleyton Hewitt.

Roddick concentrated on what he could control and gave himself the best opportunity to win. This is the mental approach the top pros take. Don't interpret this to mean that winning is not important to them. Quite the contrary, which is exactly why they try not to think about winning while they are competing.

© Lance Jeffrey

Andy Roddick concentrates on what he can control rather than worrying about the outcome of the match.

Secret 3

● *Emphasize performance goals to achieve outcome goals* ●

Setting goals is essential for anyone aspiring to reach a higher level of play. Equally important is that you understand the type of goals you are setting so that they positively affect your performance.

Performance goals are goals that you have more control over. Outcome goals are based on results, which, as you've seen, are not something you have direct control over. Ideally, if you are setting and achieving the correct performance goals, they should be helping you to achieve your outcome goals. It does not work the other way around. In other words, reaching your performance goals will give you the best chance to play up to your potential and win. Chris Carmichael, the 1999 U.S. Olympic Committee Coach of the Year and coach of cyclist Lance Armstrong, says: "It is important to set goals beyond winning and losing [performance goals] because even the most talented racers will lose more than they win."

Here are a few examples of typical performance goals. Players will have different performance goals, depending on their talent, their game, and what they need to work on to play up to their full potential. Once again, exactly what the specific performance goals are will differ for everyone, but they should be goals that help you to play your best tennis.

- I will stay in the "now" state, focusing on one point at a time.
- I will take my time between points.
- I will attack my opponent's second serve.
- I will execute the inside-out patterns that I worked on in practice.
- I will engage only in positive self-talk.

Outcome goals are also truly personal. They depend on what you want to accomplish with your tennis. Here are a few examples of outcome goals.

- Win this match
- Achieve a top-10 ranking at the club
- Win this tournament
- Beat John Doe in the league match

Secret 4

● *Cultivate intrinsic motivation and de-emphasize extrinsic motivation* ●

Similar to performance goals, you should cultivate your motivation inside yourself and not be concerned with things that lie outside yourself. Two basic sources of motivation exist: intrinsic, which comes from inside a person, and extrinsic, which comes from outside a person. In the long run, intrinsic motivation is the more powerful motivator. If you are intrinsically motivated, it means you are personally striving to master the sport or the skill at hand. The emphasis is on being the best you can be. It means you are constantly striving to improve your performance, your skills, and your mastery of the game.

Here's what Andre Agassi says about motivation: "The goal of getting better [intrinsic motivation] has to be the most important motivation because if it's to simply win a tournament [extrinsic motivation] and then you win it, what do you do then? For me, it's to see if I can play better now than I did yesterday."

Players who are intrinsically motivated develop a true passion and love for the game. Once again, the emphasis is on things you can control. Extrinsic rewards, such as trophies, victories, rankings, and public adulation, are strong motivators, but the feelings they engender tend to fade away quickly. In the long run, they are not as powerful a motivator as intrinsic ones. In addition, external motivators are the things you cannot control.

By striving for and accomplishing objectives you can control that are cultivated from within, you will derive a greater sense of satisfaction.

I believe that, if you cultivate and emphasize your intrinsic motivation and de-emphasize the extrinsic factors, it will help create a formula for you to reach your full potential. Basically, it ties right back to getting yourself psychologically into the ideal performance state. Focus on what you can control, and challenge yourself to see how well you can play and compete. People who truly strive for excellence are predominantly intrinsically motivated.

Secret 5

● *Stay in the present* ●

This is one of the keys to concentration. Learn from the past and plan for the future, but in the heat of the battle, if you are psychologically anywhere but in the present, you're in trouble. In tennis terms, this equates to playing one point at a time. Andre Agassi summed it up succinctly when he said: "I have learned the hard way that to lose the focus on one point interferes with your job. If you let up for one point, what's going to stop you from doing it on two? You can't run out the clock. You have to finish." If you catch yourself dwelling on the shot you just blew, the set you just lost, or a bad call or if you start thinking about the trophy you are about to win, you are not giving yourself the best chance to win the point you are about to play. Remember, when the point is finished, it is history. It's over, gone, and there is nothing you can do about it except move on to the next point. Is that easy to do? No. I never said it would be easy, but if you want to play your best tennis, it is a must.

> It was 1977, and I was playing in my first Wimbledon championships against a player named Freddy McNair. It had been a long, tough first-round battle. I had been down double match point in the fourth set, and now I was serving the match 5–4 in the fifth. I hit an overhead away for a winner to make the score 40–0, triple match point. I turned to my friend and quietly said, "I can't believe I am going to win this match." Guess what? Freddy hit a few winners, I made a few mistakes, and the next thing I know I had lost serve and then the match, 16–14, in the fifth set. Tough lesson. Stay in the present, and don't focus on winning or losing while you are competing.

Secret 6

● *Project a powerful, positive presence* ●

No matter what the circumstances, try to always project a powerful, positive presence on the court. That does not mean you have to be stoic because that just doesn't fit everyone's personality. You can get angry and still present a strong image. Sometimes, you will have to simply be a good actor or actress to disguise how you feel. However, never, never let someone think they are getting to you mentally. It is okay to lose the match, but don't give your opponent the satisfaction or the confidence of thinking that she has broken you down emotionally. Whether you are winning, losing, or playing someone who is simply better than you are, act confident and under control. This will leave a lasting impression on your opponent, and, many times, when you least expect it, he might be the first one to "crack" mentally. But, most important, by maintaining this type of presence, you are taking a major step in controlling your emotions.

It was 1987, during the French Junior championships. I was traveling with four junior boys, Jim Courier, Jonathan Stark, David Wheaton, and Chris Garner. Jim Courier, 17 years old at the time (and future number-one men's player in the world and two-time French Open singles champion), and Jonathan Stark (future number-one men's player in the world in doubles and French Open doubles champion) were playing in the first round of the French Junior doubles. Both boys were upset earlier in the day in the first round of the singles and, consequently, were despondent when they went on the court to play the doubles. They were playing a team from the Ivory Coast, which they should have been beating comfortably. They had just lost the first set, and boy was it ugly! Their body language was terrible, they were talking negatively after almost every point, and they looked like losers. What was even more frustrating was that we had just talked earlier before the match about forgetting about the singles loss, staying positive, and not letting their opponents know they were down. After the first set, I had decided that I would try to make a positive comment to perk them up as they came over to the side of the court where I was sitting. But before that happened, they lost serve to go down a set and a break. Jim made another negative comment and dropped his racket to the ground. I had seen enough. Jonathan glanced over at me as they started to switch sides. He knew I was fuming. Jim kept his head down and did not look. I said to Jonathan as he passed by, "One more comment out of either of you, and you are in big trouble!" and I motioned to him to get Jim's attention. Finally, Jim reluctantly looked over. "Did you hear me? One more time and big trouble!" I wasn't actually going to do anything. I just wanted to make a point. Both of them settled down, picked up their energy, started encouraging each other, and won the match in three close sets. But that was not the end of the story. They kept that positive attitude throughout the week and went on to win the tournament! They beat two great Argentineans (both were ranked in the top 100 in the world on the men's tour and still came back to play the juniors) in the finals. This was one of the most gratifying success stories of my young coaching career because I felt the boys really learned some important lessons along the way about staying in the present; using positive self-talk; and keeping a powerful, positive presence on the court. The great thing was they were rewarded for their efforts. Lesson learned!

Jonathan Stark, Nick Saviano, and Jim Courier after the boys won the French Juniors in 1987.

Secret 7

● *Engage in positive self-talk* ●

It is critical to converse with yourself in a positive way when you are on the court. Don't berate yourself or talk negatively about your game. You cannot afford to battle two opponents, the person on the other side of the net and yourself. One opponent is enough. Engaging in negative self-talk will bring you to defeat quicker than a superior opponent. If you miss an easy shot, the worst thing you can do is reinforce the mistake by verbalizing, "Oh, what an idiot I am. No way I should have missed that shot!" Instead, say something like, "You'll get it next time." Or don't say anything at all and quickly visualize yourself hitting that shot for a winner. You can even take a practice swing to imprint the positive image in your brain. Along those same lines, try to always be optimistic and think in terms of what you want to happen instead of what you don't want to happen. For example, assume you are serving for the match. During the changeover, think about wanting to hold serve and what you need to do to be successful, as opposed to thinking to yourself, "I can't lose serve now" or "Just don't miss your first serve." The point is the more you tell yourself what you don't want to happen, the more likely it is to happen. So, always think and project positively and optimistically and focus on positive affirmations.

Secret 8

● *Breathe* ●

Picture this: it is match point in the finals of the U.S. Open, and a player is about to step up to the line to serve the biggest point of her life. What is the one thing almost all players will do? Take a deep breath and exhale. Why? Because they are using their breathing as a way of helping to control themselves physically and emotionally. Controlling your breathing is one of the best ways to deal with both mental and physical anxiety. I am not advocating that you run out and take a yoga class (although that is not a bad idea). Simply remember that, by pausing and taking a deep breath between points, you can really help to control yourself. So, when you are feeling tense and uptight, stop and take a few deep breaths, and you might be surprised how much it helps.

Secret 9

● *If you can't visualize it, chances are it will not become a reality* ●

The ability to visualize yourself executing in competition is essential to achieving your goals. When top Olympic coaches and elite athletes from a wide variety of sports were surveyed as to the most important factors in their psychological training programs, they named visualization, or imagery, as number one in importance.

Try to visualize yourself performing on the court exactly the way you would like. If you have trouble with a particular shot, learn to visualize yourself hitting that shot particularly well. If you have trouble serving out a match, visualize yourself serving out the game with confidence. In preparation for a match, many professionals will actually get away by themselves shortly before competing and visualize certain aspects of the match or specific shots. Others practice their visualization at night.

It sounds corny, but for most players it really works. If you are to play in the club championships and you simply don't believe you can win it, take some time each day and visualize yourself playing the final match. Picture yourself being totally under control, executing great shots and winning the last point. The more vivid your visualization, the better. Try it, and you will be surprised just what an effective tool it is.

Secret 10

● *Maintain your routines* ●

It is critical to establish sound prepoint routines and to maintain them during competition. I am not talking about superstitions, like not stepping on the lines. Superstitions are, in my opinion, counterproductive. They are beliefs in outside sources that have nothing to do with your own ability, which will not help you during a tennis match. I am referring to the routines world-class players use to help prepare themselves physically and mentally for each point.

All players have prepoint routines whether they realize it or not. They can be something such as taking a deep breath and exhaling before you serve or looking at your strings right before you get into position to return serve. Routines help you relax, focus your concentration, and maintain the mental discipline you need during competition.

First, you should check your routines to see if they positively prepare you to play the next point. You might want to have a friend or, better yet, a certified U.S. Professional Tennis Association or Professional Tennis Registry teaching professional assess your routines to make sure that they are not excessive or drain you of energy. Second, remember to maintain these routines throughout a match. When things are going well, this is easy to do. In fact, you probably will do them without any conscious thought. However, when you are struggling, nervous, excited, upset, or simply playing poorly is when they start to go awry.

When you feel yourself emotionally out of sorts, realize that this is the time players tend to deviate from their prepoint routines. Don't let that happen. When you are out of sorts is the time you need your routines the most. Use them to help you maintain your discipline and self-control during competition. The beauty of this concept is that you are in complete control of your prepoint routines.

You should note that there are situations when you may need to adjust some of your routines. For example, if the match is not going well for you, you may want to take more time between points to slow the match down. However, occasions like that are the exception rather than the rule.

Secret 11

● *Don't make it personal* ●

Don't make your tennis match into a personal battle between you and your opponent, even if you hate his guts. It is counterproductive to focus on the person you are playing, as opposed to how he is playing, what he is doing, and what his tendencies are. If you are thinking about your opponent, you are no longer focused on your own execution.

Jennifer Capriati, after defeating Serena Williams in a hotly contested quarterfinal match at the 2001 Wimbledon, said, "I don't worry about what she [Serena Williams] is doing. I just try to concentrate on my own game." Perhaps Jim Courier said it best, just before winning the 1992 French Open: "Opponents don't worry me. It's like playing a faceless person on the other side of the net. I concentrate on me and how I play."

Secret 12

● *It's okay to be nervous; just don't be afraid* ●

In a word, I am talking about perspective. You always want to look forward to competition as a chance to challenge yourself to be your best. It is okay and normal to get nervous before and during a match. That's not such a big problem. You can learn numerous techniques to control your response, like many of the things I have discussed—positive self-talk, taking your time between points, and taking deep breaths to relax. However, you should never be afraid of competing. Simply put, being afraid means that you have things out of perspective.

All kinds of problems evolve from fear. It affects your whole system, physiological as well as psychological, from vision to breathing to coordination to concentration. Fear takes you out of the "now" state. When you are consumed with fear, you will not be able to play or think anywhere near your capabilities. And most important of all, competition is no longer fun.

Here are quotes from two great champions. Boris Becker, after losing in the first round of Wimbledon in 1987 as the defending champion, said, "Nobody died. There wasn't a war. I just lost a tennis match." Jennifer Capriati, after her semifinal loss at Wimbledon in 2001 after having won the first two Grand Slam events (Australian and French) that year said, "I just put it all in perspective, that it's really not a big deal to lose a tennis match. There are a lot worse things that could happen."

If you keep your competitive situations in perspective, you will perform better. Remember that the worst that can happen is that you lose the match.

Secret 13

● *Practice under pressure* ●

To best deal with the pressure of competition, frequently simulate those experiences in practice. The legendary coach of UCLA's dynasty, John Wooden, espoused this philosophy, "The pressure I created during practices may have exceeded that which opponents produced. I believe when an individual constantly works under pressure, they will respond automatically when faced with it during competition."

Try to duplicate the various scenarios you are faced with in match play. If you have trouble serving out a match, play some sets with a friend, where you start at 5–4 serving and then play out the set. If you don't play break points well, play a set where each game starts at break point and play out the set. Do drills where you keep the score. Play a practice set and have the loser buy lunch. If during these "pressure" situations you get nervous or don't execute well, work on applying the psychological principles in this chapter, starting with secret 1. By putting extra pressure on yourself in practice, you quickly will learn to improve your ability to execute under pressure in matches.

Remember, the biggest challenge (and the best weapon you have) when you compete comes from within your own mind. As you have read, the psychological secrets of the champions are not complicated. In fact, they are simple and easy to grasp. The difficult part is in the day-to-day application of these principles. Don't expect a metamorphosis overnight. Start with the first and most important concept of concentrating only on the things you can control. Then try to implement at least some of the principles discussed in this chapter. If you do that, you will see significant improvement over time, and your enjoyment of the game will grow exponentially.

13 Psychological Secrets of the Champions

1. Focus only on those things that you can control and disregard the rest.

2. Winning is not the number-one goal when you are competing.

3. Emphasize performance goals to achieve outcome goals.

4. Cultivate intrinsic motivation and de-emphasize extrinsic motivation.

5. Stay in the present.

6. Project a powerful, positive presence.

7. Engage in positive self-talk.

8. Breathe.

9. If you can't visualize it, chances are it will not become a reality.

10. Maintain your routines.

11. Don't make it personal.

12. It's okay to be nervous; just don't be afraid.

13. Practice under pressure.

Guarantee Success

> "Winning and losing don't always define success. Through preparation, long-term planning, and evaluation, you can improve with every match."

Wouldn't it be great to feel like you were successful in every match you played? Well, it is possible, and it is something you should strive to accomplish. Did I say winning every match? No! I said *feeling like you were success-ful*, not necessarily winning. So, what do I mean by success? I mean giving yourself the best opportunity to win and to play up to your potential. If you can accomplish this, then you truly have been successful.

Stan Smith

International Tennis Hall of Fame inductee, former No. 1 ranked men's player in the world, and Davis Cup star

Nick's concept of success is right on the mark. Many players get too absorbed in results when they should be focused on how they're developing as a player. In order to be successful you must prepare as well as you can, give the match your best effort, and honestly evaluate the match after it's over. That takes wins and losses right out of the equation—so that you truly can "guarantee" success. A close loss can provide you with extremely valuable information about your game. From that you can make improvements so you end up a much better player in the long run.

It all starts with preparation. Though I had some great results over the years, I was not the most talented player out there. To compete against the best I really had to be prepared to play. Preparation doesn't only mean getting ready for each match either. You have to consider preparation over the course of the entire season. In the off-season I used to train and compete almost as hard as the rest of the year, working with my coaches on key problems in my game and any major technique changes. That way I could start the next season with confidence. I started working on my game for the Grand Slams as early as February, March, and April so when the tournaments arrived I was ready to give them my best shot.

During the heart of the season I would look at preparation within each week, and focus on the drilling and technique work first. Then as the week progressed I would play more point situations and practice matches. Once the day of the match rolled around, I wanted my entire focus to be geared on my strategy for the match, not on technique or conditioning. Of course it was easier for me to plan my week as a pro; many players have to juggle commitments for work, school, or family. If you're pressed for time focus on only one or two things you need to work on for the next match and stick to them. Then get an objective evaluation from an outside source to view or review the match.

Before your next match take a step back and think about what you can accomplish. If you follow the steps Nick outlines in this chapter you'll go into matches with peace of mind, knowing that you're as prepared as you can possibly be. Then you can relax and enjoy the competition! Remember, only one person wins a tournament. If you improve on the areas you've identified ahead of time then your match has been an unqualified success.

Committing to Success

Too often success is equated with winning and failure with losing. While winning is one of the key barometers of success, it is not the most important one. Remember that the pursuit of simply winning is really the pursuit of mediocrity. Striving to play up to your potential and to give yourself the best chance to win is the pursuit of excellence. The commitment to personal excellence in your tennis is what will enable you to derive some success from any match, win or lose. Don't get me wrong. I understand that not everyone has endless hours to commit to his or her tennis. But these same concepts can be applied even if you have extremely limited time for your tennis. What I am encouraging you to do is to pursue excellence within the context of your ability to commit to the game. So, whether you are an aspiring professional or a weekend warrior, by applying these concepts you can achieve success and strive for excellence.

In this chapter, I will discuss the major components that go into making this commitment a reality. The competitive cycle has four components for success: preparation, competition, evaluation, and application. First, prepare for the match; then compete; then evaluate what you need to work on or improve, followed by applying any adjustments you need to make; and finally you are back to the preparation for your next match. This process can be followed even if you are playing matches every day.

Recently, I was coaching at a USA Tennis high-performance touring pro training camp. Many of the top young American professionals were there, along with two veterans, Michael Chang (former French Open champion and number two in the world) and Todd Martin (formerly top five in the world, U.S. Open finalist, and Davis Cup star). Michael and Todd are two of the brightest, most articulate, and "successful" players on the tour over the past 12 to 15 years. I say successful not just because of their on-court results but because they epitomize what it means to be committed to excellence. Year in and year out, they intuitively apply the principles of successfully completing the competitive cycle. No other players would prepare better, compete harder, analyze their performances more studiously, and then diligently work on what they deemed necessary than these two. Realizing that I had two tremendous examples of what I was trying to get across to the audience, I frequently pulled them into the discussion to draw on their vast experience. It was great because both of them kept talking about their approaches to competing— the importance of preparation, how to compete, analyzing performances, and constantly trying to improve as a player. In essence, they explained what it meant to be successful. They so powerfully reinforced to the young pros the basic concepts I was trying to convey that it really helped to make the presentation (especially after a long day of practice) a success. It also reaffirmed in my mind that the concepts I talk about in this chapter truly are a means to guarantee success in every match.

Todd Martin and Michael Chang understand the diligence and persistence required to be successful players.

Preparation

Most matches are won or lost well before you step on the court. Your preparation for a match or tournament varies significantly depending on your personal situation. Pro tennis players establish what are called periodization programs which can last up to a year. The objective of these programs is to reach a peak performance level for a few key events during the year, which for top players usually means the four major tournaments of the Grand Slam (the Australian Open, French Open, Wimbledon, and U.S. Open).

Periodization programming means organizing the training activities of an athlete so that the chances of overtraining are minimized and the chances of achieving peak performance are optimized. The periodization programs include everything from physical conditioning programs to technical stroke development. I remember in the winter of 1992 seeing Jim Courier running down the street at the Saddlebrook Resort in Florida, where he was working with his physical trainer Pat Etcheberry. I pulled the car alongside of Jim and asked him what kind of training he was doing. He said, "I am running long distances to establish my aerobic base, which is critical for me when I get over to the French." The French Open was five months away, and Courier was already starting to prepare.

In March 2000, 30 minutes after losing the finals of the Ericcson (now the NASDAQ 100) to Pete Sampras, Gustavo Kuerten was in the weight room with his coach, Larri Passos. Passos said that Gustavo was working hard on his physical strength and other aspects of his game in preparation for the French, which was still two months away. Both Courier and Kuerten were on a six-month training cycle to prepare for their biggest events. Now that's commitment!

The periodization programs the pros use generally include four phases:

1. **Phase I**—preparation phase. In this phase, players practice their tennis but don't have any tournaments coming up for a while. Typically, they work on technique or add new things to their games. They do more drilling and play fewer practice sets. They also work extremely hard physically to establish a good base of fitness.

2. **Phase II**—precompetition phase. During this phase, players are getting closer to competing. Their tournaments are usually within a week or two. The intent at this phase is to sharpen and refine tennis skills in preparation for match play. Players play a lot of point situations and practice sets as they polish their games and build confidence for the upcoming event.

3. **Phase III**—competition phase. Players are now competing in tournaments. For the pros, this phase can last months. During this phase, they employ a highly flexible training program to adjust to how they are doing in competition. For example, players will have completely different training programs if they are getting all the way to the finals of tournaments, as opposed to losing in the first rounds. The main objective of this phase is to keep tennis skills grooved, to maintain conditioning, and to prevent injuries so that they are prepared for their next match.

4. **Phase IV**—rest phase. After working so hard for so long, players need to rest and recover, both mentally and physically. Often this occurs in the off-season, when players put their rackets down and stop playing for a brief time. But rest for professional athletes means active rest. They will usually participate in some other sports or training outside of their usual tennis routines. The reason for this phase is twofold. First, it provides a physical break from the game to recover from physical fatigue and to let injured or stressed muscles heal. Second, it allows athletes to emotionally recharge their batteries to maintain their enthusiasm for the game. This is extremely important to diminish the chance of burnout after working and competing so hard.

You're probably saying, "I'm not a professional, and I don't have that kind of time or commitment." Well, that may be true, but the point is that the same basic training principles apply to all players. You can have "mini-periodization programs" that last as short as one week. Most players have at least a week of time before they play a big match or tournament. Following is a description of a one-week mini-periodization program that you can use in preparation for your next big event.

Let's assume your tournament is on Saturday and Sunday. I will start the preparation on the Monday before the match and go through each day. These suggestions are not written in stone. They are general, basic concepts to give you ideas for your own personal preparation. This sample preparation program will help you to maximize the time you do have.

All England Club (1987) during the Wimbledon Championships: MaliVai Washington, David Wheaton, Nick Saviano, Jonathan Stark, and Jim Courier. I used the basic concepts of periodization for the first time to help the boys for the International Junior Federation events with excellent success.

Monday (Active Rest or Mini-Preparation Phase)

This is a good time to review your developmental plan so that you don't get off track on what you should work on. If you have just finished a tournament on Sunday and are fatigued, this is a good day to have some active rest. Get away from tennis, take a mild jog, or do some other light exercise. If you are fresh and eager, this is a great day to work on any technical changes or refinements in your game. Work on specific patterns or anything else you feel needs to be improved in your game. Play sets if you want to, but focus more on working on your game than on being intensely competitive. You don't need or want to be razor sharp right now. Save that for the end of the week. Physically, you can train hard and push yourself because you will have time to recover.

Tuesday (Mini-Preparation Phase)

Keep working on any of the techniques, tactics, or patterns you started yesterday, but avoid tinkering with anything else or adding something new unless it is absolutely necessary. Playing points or sets is okay, but again I would emphasize working on your skills or patterns rather than competing. You don't need to be match-ready yet. You can train hard physically, but if you are fatigued from the previous day, ease up a little. There's no need to kill yourself. Your physical workouts and drilling should be short and intense. The emphasis should be on your anaerobic base because there's not enough time to significantly improve on your aerobic base. Practice visualization. Take five minutes to visualize yourself performing well, executing the shots you want, and winning points. You want positive anticipation for the competition.

Wednesday (Mini-Precompetition Phase)

Don't try to add anything new at this point because it will backfire on you during the competition. During this phase, you need to refine what you have been working on and start to sharpen up your match-play skills. This is a great day to play a competitive practice match. Playing points is also very good. If you do any drilling at all, you should use mostly live-ball, match-simulation drills. Check your equipment: rackets, shoes, clothes, water bottles, and anything else you might need for your match. It's good to plan early. Physically, you can still work hard on the court because you have plenty of time to recover. This is a great day to do a few drills to sharpen your favorite shots. You want to be supremely confident in your weapons. It is easy get caught up in other things and take your weapons for granted. That's a common, but big, mistake. After practice, get away from tennis. This will help you stay fresh. If you can, scout your opponent or get some insight into her game. Note, for example, if your opponent is left-handed or likes to serve and volley. See if you can line up a practice match with a lefty or someone who plays the same style as your opponent. You can make small adjustments in your practices, but you should stay with your basic strategy and try to impose your game on your opponent.

Thursday (Mini-Precompetition Phase)

Most of your practice should be geared toward sharpening your playing skills. Play the points and drills at full speed. Also play points and practice sets as you would want to play them in the match. By the end of the day, your equipment needs should be taken care of as best you can. You might break a string at the last minute, but there is nothing you can do about that. Make sure your rackets are strung and repaired as necessary and you have the shoes you need for the surface you're playing on. Don't leave this to the last minute so that you have to start racing around the day before the event trying to get your favorite racket strung. If you know in advance whom you are going to play, you might want to work on specific tactics that will be effective against that player (refer to chapter 3 on tactics to look at things you can do against the various types of playing styles). Practice your weapons. Hone them until they are razor sharp. Remember that this is the backbone of your confidence. Start playing the patterns and points just as you will want to play them in the match. Play a practice match or set to simulate the competition. If you know the person you're going to play, try to play with someone who has a similar style. As a general rule, you can go hard two days before a big match, but don't overdo it. At the end of this practice, your game should be sharp, and you should feel physically strong and mentally fresh.

Friday (The Day Before)

This is the day before the big match. If you can go to the site where you are playing and hit a few balls on the courts to get acclimated, it can really help. Don't practice too long. Your goal is to maintain your skills. Today is the time to ease up and have a light practice. Keep it short and simple. The primary objective is to have a short, positive workout, which leaves you feeling confident about your game as well as physically fresh. Don't dwell on the upcoming match or tournament. A lot of pros will have a quiet dinner or take in a movie simply to get away from tennis and stay mentally fresh. Pack your bag so that all your equipment is ready. Take extra rackets, an extra change of clothes, and a second pair of shoes to be safe. Pack sweats or a warm-up suit, even if it's hot outside, because you may be inside an air-conditioned room sometime during the day and you don't want to catch a chill. Also, be sure to have a water container, towel, practice balls, Band-Aids, athletic tape, sunscreen, a hat, and anything else you may need. Make sure that you have your transportation taken care of, you have directions, and you know your starting time. Line up a warm-up partner if you can. If you find that visualization works well for you, I also suggest that you spend some time visualizing yourself out on the court enjoying the competition and playing extremely well. You want positive anticipation about the match. Set up your performance goals. Remember, they should be things that you can control and that help you play up to your potential. Finally, get to bed early and get plenty of rest.

Competition

This is the big day—match day! To make everything go right, your goal is to have as few distractions as possible and have a relaxed buildup to the match.

- If you have an early-morning match, get up at least three hours before the match, have a good breakfast, and make sure you drink plenty of fluids. It is critical to be fully hydrated before you go out to play.

- Avoid reading and watching TV, which can fatigue your eyes. Everything you do should be positive, relaxing, and fun.

- Double-check your bag to make sure you have everything you need.

- Arrive early. You never want to be rushed before a match. If you live close by, you should be at the site an hour before the match. If it's a long drive, think in terms of two hours ahead. This will give you enough time to stretch out after the car ride, have an easy warm-up, and take a relaxing shower if you choose.

- Be cognizant of the weather and how it might affect your preparation and the match. For example, if it is stiflingly hot, you might want to take a shorter warm-up.

- Make sure you are drinking adequate amounts of water to keep you hydrated during your warm-up. Also, about an hour before your match is a good time to have a sport drink. This will help replace fluids and provide you with the electrolytes and carbohydrates you need for a tough match in the heat.

- Go through your normal warm-up routine. Exercise to break a sweat before you hit any balls, and start out slow. Remember, your goal is not to win the warm-up; it is to get prepared to play the match.

- Change clothes after you hit unless you are about to play in a few minutes. Don't sit around in sweaty clothes. At many tournaments, you have to wait for a significant amount of time between your warm-up and your match time. Take a quick shower if you can, get into some dry clothes, and keep yourself warm. Don't sit around in an air-conditioned room unless you put on your sweats, or you will get stiff.

- Relax. As the match approaches, do something that relaxes you. Each person is different, so you need to find what works for you. Many players choose just to have some quiet time to themselves. This will give you a chance to go over your performance goals and game plan, and get prepared mentally. It is also a good time to do some visualization. Young American star Andy Roddick, after winning the 2001 Legg Mason Tennis Classic in Washington, D.C., said: "I'm pretty focused five to ten minutes before the match begins. I get mellow, zoned in. It just happens." Other players choose to talk with friends about other sports, politics, or anything to keep their minds off the match. Many listen to music. Do whatever works best for you. The bottom line is that you should be relaxed and mentally positive right before you go out to play.

• Don't talk about your tennis with anyone except your coach right before you go out for the match. Talking with others about your tennis can get you obsessed or worried and will usually backfire on you.

• If you get a chance to watch your opponent hit before your match, that's fine, but only watch for a few minutes and only to specifically find out things about his game. Don't read too much into what you see. John McEnroe was one of the worst warm-up players I ever saw. Once a match started, however, John was a different player. Don't ask a lot of people about your opponent's game. Usually, they'll overestimate or underestimate your opponent's ability.

• Project confidence. Think powerful, positive presence. Sport psychologist Father Joe Dispenza once told me, with a bit of tongue-in-cheek, "Nick, there are two ways to walk around the tournament site—like you own the place or you are looking to buy it." You get the point.

John McEnroe was not a great practice player but in competition it was another story!

© Associated Press

• Look forward to the challenge of competing and don't try to guarantee a win. Just focus on what you can control and play one point at a time.

You are now officially ready to play. You have had a great week of practice, and you've done everything right in your prematch warm-up. Now enjoy the match!

Evaluation

An important part of making every match you play a success is learning from the battle. Try to be objective about the match. Don't get too high about winning, and, conversely, don't get too down about losing. Your goal is to get good, sound information about your match that can help you improve. Here are a few helpful hints on how to achieve a good postmatch evaluation.

• **Allow yourself an emotional cooldown.** Allow yourself to cool down emotionally before you get feedback or do a self-analysis. For some people, that can be five minutes; others may need an hour or two. However, the sooner you start getting or giving yourself some good feedback, the better.

• **Review performance goals.** Take some time to review your goals for the match and see how you did. Here are three questions you should ask yourself: What did I do well? Start with the positive. Remember, you should derive some degree of success even from a losing situation. I don't care if you played what you think is the worst match of your life. There were some positives about what happened on the court. Acknowledge those and learn from them. What broke down? These might be areas in which you normally do well, but for some reason they broke down during the match. What are my areas of deficiency? These are areas that consistently caused you trouble.

• **Get a coach's perspective.** If possible, get your teaching pro to watch your match, even if you have to pay a fee. The feedback your pro can give you because he knows your game will be one of the most valuable lessons you can receive.

• **Get your opponent's perspective.** Often, your opponent will give you some valuable insights into how you played, what was effective, and what was not. Ask questions and listen.

• **Get outside feedback.** Sometimes a friend who has watched you play—especially one with a knowledge of the game—can give you some good, basic feedback.

• **Watch the stats.** Statistics, such as first-serve percentage, unforced errors, winners, and break points, can be extremely helpful. Statistics alone, however, can be misleading. For example, you might have gotten 80 percent of your first serves in and committed no double faults, which sounds impressive. But if you were just softly lofting both serves into the court, such high percentages might not have done you any good. There's an old saying to keep in mind: "There are lies, there are damn lies, and there are statistics."

• **Take notes.** It sounds corny, but for most players it works. You will be amazed at how much you forget even after one day.

After you have gotten some good feedback and done some self-analysis, you can determine the areas you need to work on to improve your game. Look for trends from previous matches. If you are consistently having the same problem with one aspect of your game, that is something you will want to address in practice. Be sure not to overreact to a bad performance. It may have been just an off day. For example, if you missed a lot of backhands, don't all of a sudden think you need to switch from a two-handed backhand to a one-hander. Now, you are ready to apply what you have learned.

Application

To complete the process of guaranteeing success, you must apply what you have learned from competition and incorporate that into your practice program. Then it becomes part of your preparation for your next competition.

Let's assume the technique on your serve kept breaking down. The result was a lot of double faults. On Monday, you might ask a local pro to give your serve the once-over. Then you could practice the "new technique" for a day or two by hitting a few extra baskets of balls and playing practice points where you only get one serve, to help the execution and confidence of your second serve. Finally, play some intense practice matches to gauge how the serve holds up.

During the match, maybe you were tactically confused on where to hit the volley when you came into the net. Sit down with a pro or watch a world-class player on TV to see what kind of patterns and shot selections she plays when she comes to the net. Then pick out a frequent pattern you play when you come to the net. Let's say you like to hit your forehand down the line to your opponent's backhand and come in. Go out with a friend and walk through the different scenarios. If she hits the pass down the line, volley to the open court. If she hits the pass crosscourt, volley either down the line or back behind him. After that, practice hitting forehand approach shots, come to the net, and play out the point. Practice this pattern in drills and point situations, then practice matches. Now you can incorporate this pattern into a match.

Those are just a few examples of how to apply some of the information you get from evaluating your match performance. But whatever system you use, apply to your practice program what you have learned from the match. If you don't, you will simply make the same mistakes match after match and you will be frustrated and upset.

By applying the principles of preparation, evaluation, and application with the competition concepts I have discussed throughout this book, you will be giving yourself the best chance to win and to play up to your maximum potential, which I said earlier is a formula for guaranteeing success every time you compete. Each practice will become more purposeful. It will become exciting when you see your rate of improvement accelerate beyond what you thought was possible. So, complete the competitive cycle, and guarantee success the next time you compete!

Synergize in Doubles

> Make a successful transition from singles to doubles by creating synergism in communication, movement, positioning, and strategy.

Have you ever watched two players who are truly outstanding in doubles, yet not nearly as good in singles? They may not seem to have many outstanding weapons. They aren't overpowering or flashy. Their styles may be completely different. Their personalities may be the antitheses of each other, yet they play incredible doubles together.

What you are seeing is the creation of synergism on the tennis court. Two players combine their separate abilities with superb communication and movement skills to produce a doubles team better than the sum of its parts. It's a beautiful thing to watch at every level of the game, from the local club level to the Grand Slam events.

Pam Shriver

International Tennis Hall of Fame inductee and winner of 21 Grand Slam doubles titles

Synergy is a perfect term to articulate what you need to accomplish in doubles. When I played with Martina Navratilova we won 20 Grand Slam titles. We made a great pair because we were truly a "team" on the court. We had wonderful synergy. She was a left-handed, shot making, power player, with the flair for the dramatic. I was the right-handed, steady, percentage player that looked to set up her partner rather than go for a lot of the winners. We complemented each other perfectly.

Martina was an incredible singles player (maybe the best ever) but there's hardly a guarantee that putting two good singles players together will result in a winning tandem. Often, the exact opposite is true. Many singles players are too used to being in a much more independent state. They're self-reliant. They don't know how to build a relationship, both mental and physical, with a partner on the court. However, in doubles, the sum is always greater than the two individual parts. That's why you'll see two great singles paired together for something special like Davis or Fed Cup, or a Grand Slam, get bumped off by a seasoned and complementary team of lesser individual talent.

That's not to say that a player more into their singles game can't excel, enjoy, and improve their overall game by engaging in doubles. In fact, from a physical standpoint, a player can only help their singles game by playing doubles, and emotionally it can be a real plus. Players that are too narrowly focused and uptight about their tennis can find a real balance in doubles. Playing doubles allows for more of your personality to manifest on the court. It did for me and that's why I, personally, think you can have more fun playing doubles. So much of that has to do with your partner. You've got to find a partner who clicks with you on the court. It doesn't always happen right away, and it doesn't happen with every player. That is what I like about this chapter. Nick not only addresses the fundamentals of movement and tactics, which when I was playing my best were the things I did well, but he talks about the golden rules for picking a partner and building a good relationship. Above all, when you're playing doubles, don't forget to smile and have an occasional laugh on the court. It's is a great way to break the tension and help you to fully enjoy and appreciate doubles tennis.

Creating Synergism

Synergism is the interaction of elements that when combined produce a total effect that is greater than the sum of the individual elements. That is in essence what you want to achieve on the court when you play doubles. The goal of this chapter is to help you create that wonderful experience.

Numerous factors go into creating synergism on the court. Of course, you need to have good tactics and racket skills. However, many great players are well versed in doubles tactics and are great hitters of the ball, yet they don't make a good partner in doubles. Real synergism takes much more than simply knowing how and where to hit the ball. The key is in the relationship between the partners.

Before you can expect to create true synergism on the court, you must follow some golden rules in building a good doubles relationship. Most of these rules apply even if you are playing a pickup game. They help to establish good karma on the court, which is a prerequisite to creating synergism.

Picking the Right Partner

Number one, naturally, is to pick the right partner. That's not as easy as it sounds. The obvious move, choosing the best tennis player you can get, may not be your best bet; compatibility between partners may be more important. How do you find the right partner? You must keep many things in mind, such as commitment, game style, respect, honesty, and self-awareness, as well as the more practical elements such as schedules and being able to communicate.

PHILOSOPHICAL APPROACH AND COMMITMENT

You don't have to have the same personality as your partner. You don't have to be best friends. However, it is important to have a similar level of commitment and competitiveness. If you're going to play a tournament and you prepare diligently to do as well as you can but your partner doesn't have the same commitment you do, then you are going to have all kinds of problems. If you are playing with someone who has the same competitive fire as you do, it helps to build a bond of mutual respect, even if you have nothing in common off the court.

COMPLEMENTARY GAME STYLE

Try to find a player who possesses skills or weapons that you might not have. For example, if you have a huge serve but poor returns, it would be advantageous to get a partner with a good return. Two players with bad returns on a team is a formula for disaster. If that partner also happens to have a good serve, as well, all the better.

RESPECT AND HONESTY

Whether you are playing socially or seriously in tournaments, play with someone you respect and enjoy being with on the court. That doesn't mean that you have to go out to dinner with this person. However, if you don't enjoy being around her, your doubles partnership won't be a success. And remember to always show respect for your partner. Be sensitive to her feelings. That supersedes all other considerations.

Part of respect is honesty, so give an honest assessment of your game. This goes hand in hand with self-awareness. Park your ego at the practice court, and accurately acknowledge what your strengths and weaknesses are. By honestly assessing your playing skills, you'll make it a lot easier to develop a winning strategy with your partner. Also, give an honest assessment of your partner's game. This is a sensitive area, so let her tell you where her strengths and weaknesses lie. Often, a big gap exists between perception and reality. Don't confront the discrepancy; instead, be considerate but make a realistic strategic plan.

Pam Shriver and Martina Navratilova—one of the greatest doubles teams ever to play.

© Lance Jeffrey

When I was playing my last year as an amateur, I played doubles with a guy named Peter. He was a good player, but I wasn't sure he had a big-time future in professional tennis. As a team, we finished our junior career ranked third in the United States and won the U.S. National Amateur Clay Court championships the following year. Nevertheless, I decided, in my infinite wisdom, that I needed to play with someone who would become a big-time player on the pro tour. So, I decided not to play with Peter anymore.

A few years later, at the French Open, I was sitting in the lounge of the Sofitel hotel in Paris with an 18-year-old from New York named John. I had known John since he was 12 years old, having stayed at his house for a junior event years earlier. He was the top American junior at the time and was scheduled to play the qualifying tournament for the main draw of the French Open, as well as the French Juniors event. As he was pacing in the lounge, he asked me about the possibility of playing with him in a professional event in Newport, Rhode Island, the week after Wimbledon. I was ranked high enough on the pro tour to get into the main draw of that tournament, but he did not have a ranking. He said he needed to get some ATP (Association of Tennis Professionals) points so that he could get his ranking up. He believed that he could get a wild card into the main draw. I told him that it was a possibility but that I was not sure and I had to see how things went at Wimbledon. One thing led to another, and I never firmed up that offer from John.

Well, guess what? That young man qualified for the French Open, teamed up with Mary Carrillo to win the French Open mixed doubles title, and two weeks later qualified for and reached the semifinals of Wimbledon. Of course, I am talking about John McEnroe. To add insult to injury, he teamed up with the player I used to play doubles with, and John McEnroe and Peter Fleming became one of the greatest doubles teams ever.

SCHEDULING AND COMMUNICATION

Pick someone who can play a comparable schedule and with whom you easily communicate. If your partner can't play when and where you can, you're wasting your time. Be aware of your own idiosyncrasies and needs on the court. I'm talking about things such as how you respond to pressure situations, how you handle criticism, and what kind of nonverbal messages you send out. Being aware of them, you can either make adjustments to change them if you know they'll annoy your partner or inform him of them so that he will know what to expect from you. This is a prerequisite to good communication. It is also important to know your partner's idiosyncrasies. How does she respond under pressure? How much does she like to talk during the match? Does she need constant encouragement? How does she respond to criticism? What are her preferences in terms of shots? If you know these things about your partner, you will be able to develop excellent communication—or decide that you don't want to play with her.

Communication

One of the most important components of a successful doubles team is effective communication. Armed with the knowledge about yourself and your partner, you now have created the environment to establish excellent communication. Remember that good communication takes a real commitment and doesn't happen overnight. But it is definitely worth the effort and the time. Here are some tips to creating good communication. They may sound like things you hear in marriage counseling, but they do work.

Tips for Strong Communication

- Be supportive and understanding. This is especially important when things are not going well. Remember, sometimes it does not pay to be honest. For example, if your partner has missed every break-point return, you don't need to tell him that. Keep encouraging him instead.

- Build confidence. Compliment your partner frequently. Whether it is a good shot or a good decision, it never hurts. Be positive and upbeat. Remember, you are a team and you need one another to succeed. Building your partner's confidence will yield positive results.

- Enjoy yourself. Show your partner that you are enjoying playing with her and having fun in the competition. Nothing makes your partner relax more than when she sees that you are relaxed and enjoying yourself.

- Establish your communication style. Because every player has different personal preferences, every doubles team will have their own communication style. Some will talk a great deal and at every opportunity, while others seem to communicate simply with gestures or nods. You must figure out what works best for you.

Todd Woodbridge and Mark Woodford know what it takes to make a great doubles team.

Recently, at a practice session before a professional event in Delray Beach, I asked Todd Woodbridge what made him and Mark Woodford such a special team. "Sure, doubles is a matter of teamwork, but it's more than that. It is a matter of having the same philosophy about what you are trying to achieve. That is why Mark and I go so well together. Obviously, we both wanted to play well individually, but we were happy to help each other play well. That meant setting the play up for each other, not just trying to be an individual trying to hit a winner. On the returns, we were happy to put the ball in solid and let the net man do the work. Mark and I communicated extremely well. That is what sets up great plays on the court." (Woodbridge and Woodford won 11 Grand Slam titles together.)

There are three key phases in the communication process of a match: before the match, during the match, and after the match. Here are some basic fundamentals of communication for each phase that should be considered by everyone who wants to create synergism with his partner on the court.

COMMUNICATION BEFORE THE MATCH

Prior to the beginning of a match, especially if you haven't played much with each other, you should go over everything you need to know for your match. Practicing together before your match provides a good opportunity to do this. Otherwise, sit down with each other and discuss specifics about your opponent and your game plan for the match. Decide the style of communication you will use during the match. For example, do you want to use hand signals for poaching, or will you communicate that verbally? If there are some extenuating circumstances, make sure you inform your partner now, as opposed to during the match. For example, if you have a sore shoulder that is affecting your serve, tell your partner, and maybe she will be more aggressive at the net when you are serving, to take the pressure off of you. The more you understand what to expect from each other, the better chance you have of playing great doubles. This will help you get in sync and flow as a team.

COMMUNICATION DURING THE MATCH

Communication during a match happens between points, during points, and during the changeover. Your communication patterns may differ from other teams. Some teams will use hand signals, some will speak to each other frequently, and some teams will have far fewer planned tactics and just respond instinctively during play. The point is that you must find what works best for you. The rising young American team of Mike and Bob Bryan speak after virtually every point about tactics, whereas the record-setting team of Pam Shriver and Martina Navratilova did not speak nearly as often. American Davis Cup heroes Ken Flach and Robert Seguso used to signal each other where they were going to serve and whether they were going to poach.

The most important thing is to be positive, encouraging, and upbeat. Remember that nonverbal communication can be as effective or damaging as the spoken word. A nod of encouragement or a disgusted shake of the head sends a powerful message. Always assume that your partner has eyes in the back of his head. Don't let your frustrations show when you think your partner is not looking. Stay positive. A pump of the fist, a high five, a pat on the back, or simply a big smile goes a long way to boost your partner.

The best time to make any significant tactical adjustments during a match is during the changeover between games. This is the time you get to sit down together, so you can have a quick discussion about what is happening and how to respond.

Between points is when you should let your partner know what you intend to do during the next point. For example, if you are going to hit the return down the line or you are going to poach if you're at the net, let your partner know. When you are serving, let your partner know what type of serve you're going to hit and where you intend to hit it so that he can be

© Cynthia Lum

Mike and Bob Bryan talk strategy after nearly every point in a match.

better prepared and position himself properly. When your partner is returning serve, tell him that you intend to poach if the return is hit down low at your opponent's feet. Between points is also the time to encourage each other or acknowledge a good shot.

Good teams also communicate during a point when the situation warrants it. For example, if your partner covers a lob over your head, she should say "switch" to remind you to cross over to cover her side of the court. If you're about to hit a defensive lob, you should say something like "back" so that your partner can move back from the net. It's also important to call out "mine" or "yours" when your opponent hits a lob or other shot that's difficult to reach or not clearly in either of your territories.

Regardless of what style of communication you have, the intent is to build a sense of teamwork while on the court. So, always be positive and work with your partner.

As a young touring professional, I was playing in the South African Open when Bob Hewitt—one of the all-time great doubles players who usually partnered with Frew McMillan—asked me to play doubles with him. I couldn't believe it! Bob had won nine Grand Slam doubles titles and was formerly ranked number one in the world in doubles. Unfortunately, I was nervous during the match and did not play well (neither did Bob). We lost in the first round, which I am sure was as disappointing for Bob as it was for me. But what stood out in my mind and impressed me the most that day was that, as great a doubles player as Bob was and as bad as I played that day, he never said or did anything to make me feel like it was my fault or that he was unhappy to play with me. That made a real impression on me . . . but he never did ask me to play with him again!

COMMUNICATION AFTER THE MATCH

Talking with your partner after the match is over is just as important to building a good team as communicating during the match. Here are some guidelines for communicating with your partner after a match.

1. **The sooner the better.** As a general rule, it is better to talk about the match shortly after playing while the match is fresh in your mind. However, use common sense. If you just lost a heartbreaker, it may be best to let things calm down before you discuss what happened.

2. **Start with the positive.** Nothing will turn your partner off quicker than saying something negative about the match, even if it's true. Remember, you want to build up your partnership, not tear it down. So start with what went well.

3. **Critique yourself, not your partner.** Actually, something that will turn your partner off more quickly than saying something negative about the match is saying something negative about him. Always review what your team did well together, and if you have to bring up anything negative, make sure you do it about your faults or use the word "we" if you are discussing something your partner did. For example, "We did not poach enough today," as opposed to "You didn't poach enough." Win or lose, if your partner starts to feel that you are frustrated or unhappy playing with her, you can kiss the synergism good-bye.

4. **Analyze your tactics.** Make sure you discuss how well you executed your game plan and what adjustments you might need to make to counter what happened in the match. Also review the things you may need to practice for the next match.

5. **If you win . . .** After a win, everyone is usually very happy, which makes this a great time for constructive criticism or to address other sensitive issues that have been bugging you. If you do this after you've lost, the danger exists that your partner may feel that you blame him for the loss or that what is bothering you is not real because you are upset over losing.

6. **If you lose . . .** Don't express frustration at your partner's play. Do not blame your partner. I don't care if your partner blew every easy sitter or did not hold serve all day. Let your partner know that you enjoyed playing with her. If she played poorly and cost you the match, she knows that and probably feels bad enough. Say something to the effect that it's okay. The last thing you want is your partner to sense that you don't want to play with her. That only will make her nervous during matches, and you'll never create a good synergism.

Tactics

Sound tactics are critical to success in doubles at any level. A doubles team who employs excellent tactics will beat a far superior team (as far as tennis skills and ability are concerned) who uses poor tactics. The bottom line is, the use of flawed tactics can sink any doubles team regardless of ability. Following is a list of the key tactical principles for great doubles. Follow these golden rules and execute well, and you'll ascend to heights you didn't know you were capable of reaching.

- **Keep it basic and simple.** As with singles, the tactics you apply in doubles should be simple, with the emphasis on executing well. Even the most clever or elaborate tactics are futile if you can't execute them well.

- **Maximize your strengths and minimize your weaknesses.** Any tactics you employ should highlight your strengths and hide your weaknesses. For example, if you have a great serve, make sure you serve first at the start of every set. If you have a weak backhand return, stand over to the backhand side on second serves, and bait your opponent into hitting to your forehand.

- **Simplify choosing sides.** Don't make choosing which side of the court you are going to play too complicated. As a general rule, simply play the side that gives you the opportunity to hit more of your favorite shots. For example, if you have a lot of confidence in your forehand and are right-handed, you probably want to play in the deuce court.

- **When serving, think high percentages.** This is very important because you need to give your team the chance to win points. If you don't get in a high percentage of your first serves, your opponents will be looking at second serves all day. That will neutralize your partner at the net, and you'll find yourself hitting volleys off your shoe tops or watching winners zip by you.

- **Hit good returns.** If you don't make the return or you give your opponents easy sitters, the point is over. It is critical to get the ball in play. Hitting one screaming winner and four errors is not going to help your team. Your first goal is to make the return. Your second goal is to get the ball down low at your opponents' feet. If you do that frequently, your partner will look like a star as he knocks off the weak replies from your opponents. If you get a high percentage of first serves in and a lot of returns down low, you will win a lot of matches.

- **Make first volleys.** Just as on serves and returns, it is critical to make the first volley. It does not have to be a great volley all the time because your team will have two people covering the net. Too often players let the opponent at the net distract them. They worry that this player will cross to poach their shot, and as a result they miss the volley. Don't worry about your opponent. Simply decide where you are going to hit the first volley, and then just hit it. Even if your opponent guesses correctly, she still has to make the shot.

- **Think offensively.** Doubles is an offensive game that usually rewards the aggressive team. I am not talking about teeing off on every shot. The goal is to constantly try to create an offensive situation either through positioning or the quality of your shots. Unlike in singles, where a good counterpuncher can have significant success, high-percentage, controlled aggression rules the doubles court.

- **Play back.** If your team is having trouble returning, try having both of you stay back. This is a good defensive tactic when your team can't get effective returns in the court. It will give your team more margin for error on the returns and also help neutralize your opponent at the net. With both of you back, it's not as easy to put the ball away on a poach as it would be if one of you stayed close to the net. This simple tactic can change the whole complexion of a match by forcing your opponents to adjust tactically and improving your chances of getting the return in play.

- **Remember, power is not everything.** In today's game of power tennis, don't be sucked into the mentality that everything needs to be hit hard. A medium-paced shot, low over the net, is still incredibly effective in doubles because it forces your opponents to hit up, giving your team a chance for a put-away. Sometimes a blocked return, hit softly at the feet, is far better than a 100-mile-per-hour screamer.

- **Use the lob as a weapon.** Most people realize how important a good defensive lob is when you are hopelessly out of position and just trying to stay in the point. However, in doubles the lob should be used as a weapon, as well. It's a means to neutralize the net person from poaching, keep her from getting too close to the net, expose a weak overhead, blind your opponent by hitting the lob into the sun, lob over their heads to take control of the net, and sometimes to simply win the point outright. So, remember, think of the lob as a potential weapon.

- **Challenge the net player.** On return games, challenge the person at the net right away. Lob him, hit right at him, or go down his line within the first two return games. This will keep him guessing throughout the match and less likely to cross over and poach.

- **Create two-shot winners.** You don't have to win every point with one shot. Try to set up your partner by hitting a good, low return, a well-placed serve, or a deep volley. You don't have to do it all. Remember, doubles is a team game.

- **Don't be a court hog.** Don't forget that your primary responsibility is to cover your half of the court. Constantly roaming too far to take balls that you shouldn't will open up holes in your area.

- **Be decisive.** Being tentative in doubles is the kiss of death. If you are going to poach, then go. If the ball is hit up the middle, go for it. There's no time to be indecisive. Doubles is a high-intensity, aggressive game.

- **Employ the center theory.** As a general rule in doubles, when in doubt, play the ball back low and toward the center of the court. That way the ball travels over the lowest part of the net, cuts down on the angles your opponent can hit, and gives your team an opportunity to stay in the point.

- **Create angles.** Ideally you want to hit shots that eventually will give you easy balls to angle off of or put away. Conversely, don't give your opponents angles unless you have put them in a defensive position. For example, if you hit down the line, you'd better hit an aggressive shot. If your shot is short or sits up, you give your opponents an opportunity to hit a sharp angle or play it up the middle or down the line. All of a sudden, you and your partner are forced to defend a larger area. The point is not to open up the court until you are ready to finish the point. Create angles; don't give them to your opponents.

- **Smile.** Having fun is a key to success. Sometimes a "well-timed" smile or a laugh is a good tactic to break the tension in a big match. So, if things are getting tight out there, try a big smile to loosen things up

Movement

Watching a good doubles team move is like watching a couple dance. They each seem to know exactly what the other person is going to do, they each know exactly where they need to be, and they move in unison. It takes time and practice to acquire this type of movement proficiency, but you can cut the learning curve by remembering a few basic concepts—moving together, staying in position, and predicting upcoming moves.

MOVE AS A UNIT

Doubles is a fast-moving, dynamic game that requires your team to move together as much as possible. When one of you takes the offensive, the other should, too. The best offensive position is with both of you at the net. So, if your partner is at the net, you should try to get in, too. If one of you is in a defensive position, you should assume a defensive position, as well. The strongest defensive position is with both players in the backcourt. Good doubles is a constant transitioning back and forth, from offensive to defensive, as both teams maneuver to try to take the net and win the point. The idea is to be on the offensive as much as possible. The worst scenario is for your team to stay in the one-up, one-back position, with which you start off every point. If you are at the net and your partner stays back, you might get your head knocked off if your partner hits a weak reply. At the very least, that positioning opens up too many opportunities for your opponents to put the ball away.

GET IN A GOOD POSITION

Good movement in doubles means constantly moving as a unit based on the position of the ball on your opponents' side of the net. Ideally, you and your partner should stay a comfortable distance apart to protect the middle, while still being able to cover as much of the rest of the playing area as possible. The middle is determined by the location of the ball on your opponents' side of the court. If the ball is in the middle of the court, then your middle is right down the center of the court. If the ball is wide in the deuce court, your team needs to shift in unison to the left to cover the most probable angles. The idea is to minimize the holes in your defense.

BE PREDICTABLE TO YOUR PARTNER

Always let your partner know when you are going to move or understand where you will be in a given situation. Good doubles teams look as if they have mental telepathy. Conversely, you want to keep your opponents constantly off balance and guessing as to when you will move and where you will wind up. Be predictable to your partner and unpredictable to your opponents.

Everybody should play at least some doubles because it can be a real blast. The way to get the most enjoyment from the game, to play your best and achieve the best results, is to create synergism with your partner. Complement your skills, communicate together, remember some basic golden rules, and together you'll find you can take your game to new levels. So, pick out a good partner; work on the concepts discussed in this chapter; and see your results skyrocket, along with your excitement for the game.

10

Play From the Heart

> "Fun and enjoyment of the game are the foundation from which everything grows. Follow these steps to free your game to reach its potential."

Reflect for a moment on a time when you played your best tennis. Perhaps it was a victory over the number-one player at your club or when you won a big tournament. Or maybe it was a losing effort against a superior opponent. How did you perceive your tennis at that time? Did you look forward to playing? Was the match fun and enjoyable? I would be willing to bet the answer is yes. In all of my years of playing and coaching, I can't remember hearing a player say, "I hated being out on the court today, but I just had the best win of my life." You'll rarely hear someone say, "Practice has been miserable, but, wow, am I improving!" It is ludicrous to think you can improve your tennis when you are devoid of fun, enjoyment, and passion for the game. If fact, without it, your chances of taking your game to the next level are virtually nil.

Billie Jean King

International Tennis Hall of Fame inductee and winner of 39 Grand Slam titles

I absolutely agree with the principles of this chapter that having fun and enjoyment with your tennis is a key to reaching your full potential. From the first day I picked up a racquet I loved to play. And even now at 58, I still can't get enough of it. It used to be my stage when I was a professional player. I love how my mind has to connect with my body. It's an opportunity to forget everything else going on in my life for a moment, and do something just for me. Basically I just love tennis.

In order to be your best at something, you've got to love it. Going out on the court, working hard, and practicing your game shouldn't seem like work at all. In fact, it's got to be fun. Otherwise improvement will be a difficult thing to achieve. I wouldn't have been nearly as successful in my career if I didn't possess a passion for the game. For example, the great Boris Becker is remembered as being a phenomenal talent, but the German Tennis Federation didn't always see it that way. As a child, they had extremely low expectations for Becker because he didn't test well in areas like quickness and vertical leap. But as far as enjoyment and motivation, he was off the charts! So they decided to keep him around and let him practice with the girls, which was considered a kind of insult. Except one of those little girls happened to be Steffi Graf and the two of them pushed each other toward greatness. I saw it firsthand on the Wimbledon practice courts. I stopped my workout (which I normally never did) because I had to see who this kid was on the next court playing with such fire and passion. You could just feel his presence and his joy to be out there. Two years later he was the Wimbledon champion. The rest is history.

Having Becker-like ability or not, in order for you to continually grow as a tennis player, you've got to thoroughly enjoy being out on the court and expanding your limits. It has to be fun. That's why this chapter is so important—it shows you how to enhance the things you love to do on the court and minimize the things you don't. For most people, playing tennis is not their job. It's not something they have to do. So if you're going to give up some of your precious free time to do it, you might as well enjoy it! I guarantee that if you enjoy it, you can't help but improve.

Before the start of the 1999 Wimbledon final against Andre Agassi, Pete Sampras told his coach, Paul Annacone, that "this is going to be fun. I'm going to enjoy this time. Who knows how many more finals I'll play here and how often I'll play Andre?" That same year Steffi Graf was coming back from an injury and unexpectedly won the French Open. Three short weeks later, she lost in the finals of Wimbledon to Lindsay Davenport and announced that it would be her last Grand Slam event. "The last few weeks have been pretty amazing," Graf said. "It's obvious that I'm disappointed about losing the final, but I do have to say it's been great. . . . It's been a lot of fun." After losing in the 2001 Wimbledon final, 9–7, in the fifth set, the great Australian Patrick Rafter said, "It was electric out there, that is what we play for, it was a lot of fun."

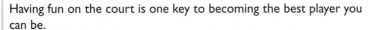

Having fun on the court is one key to becoming the best player you can be.

Sure you say. Those players have won millions of dollars playing tennis and can afford to say that it's fun. But do you really think they would have endured countless hours of training and practicing, overcome agonizing injuries, and struggled to gain their successes over the years if it wasn't fun and enjoyable to be on the court? Tennis can be hard work, and it takes sacrifice to reach your potential at almost every level. If you do not enjoy your time spent on the court, the rewards are often not enough to keep you playing tennis.

Tennis is a game and as such should be fun and enjoyable, which over time will manifest itself into a real passion for the game. The love of the game is a key ingredient to your success in tennis. Of course, tennis has become many other things in today's world. It can be an avenue to fame and fortune for those good enough to compete at the highest level. It can be the means to earning a living for players, coaches, manufacturers, entrepreneurs, administrators, and business people. It can be the path to college scholarships. It can be a proving ground for your self-worth—your standing in your peer group, club, or community. And it is a wonderful way to keep physically fit. But first and foremost, tennis is a game, a wonderful game for a lifetime, from which we should derive enjoyment.

The principle of having fun and cultivating not only a love but also a true passion for tennis is a prerequisite to any meaningful and significant improvement in your game. If you don't enjoy your time on the court, whether it's in practice or in competition, you might as well kiss success good-bye. This is true for every tennis player—a world-class professional, a college player, an aspiring junior, or a recreational player. We've all heard great athletes from every sport say things like, "I play because I love the game," or a veteran who states, "I play because I still have a passion and enjoyment for the competition," or the idol of millions who claims, "Playing this game is not work for me. It's fun." The message is so loud that it's deafening, yet it is consistently overlooked and misinterpreted.

Questions to Ask

I have had the opportunity and privilege over the years, first as a private coach and later as a coach with the U.S. Tennis Association's player development and high-performance program, to work with hundreds of top players at the junior, collegiate, and world-class level. When players have problems with their games, I am often asked by the players, their parents, or their personal coaches to analyze their game. The first thing I assess is their state of mind. I ask two simple questions: "Are you having fun and enjoying yourself when you play tennis?" and "What is preventing you from getting pleasure out on the court?"

In 1990, I was at the All-England Championships at Wimbledon, as the national coach of the U.S. Tennis Association's player development program. I was talking with a young touring pro, named Jim, with whom I had worked in years past at numerous international junior events. He was 19 years old, a product of the Nick Bollettieri Tennis Academy, and one of the top young prospects in the world. He had been struggling lately and asked me if I would watch his first-round match and tell him what the problem might be. As I watched him play, it became apparent that he was extremely uptight and tense. Playing seemed like a burden to him. He was totally devoid of joy on the court.

Not surprisingly, he was soundly beaten. After the match, I said, "Jim, you are so tense out there that any tactical or technical suggestions I might have won't provide much benefit at this point. First, you must focus on relaxing on the court and enjoying competing and practicing. Only then will you be able to incorporate the necessary adjustments in your game."

Grand Slam title winner Jim Courier understands the necessary balance between intensity and relaxation.

© Associated Press

(continued next page)

(continued from previous page)

He understood what I was getting at. True to his incredible work ethic and determination, Jim left no stone unturned as he set out to find a balance of intensity, relaxation, and enjoyment in his tennis. Under the excellent guidance of his coaches, Jose Higueras and Brad Stine, Jim continued to develop his game and found the balance he needed to allow him to enjoy playing and truly develop his great potential.

Eleven months later, Jim won the 1991 French Open singles title, the first of his four Grand Slam titles, and became the number one-ranked player in the world. Until the day he retired, he was recognized as one of the tour's great competitors and among the finest "big-match" players in the game. Of course, I am talking about the great Jim Courier.

When a player is struggling, the answer to the first question is usually a resounding no. Once it is apparent what is obstructing her from enjoying her tennis experience, as determined by the answer to the second question, it is relatively easy to map out a strategy for getting her back on the right track.

Most players (and unfortunately many parents of young players) have a difficult time accepting the fundamental principle of fun. Often, "serious" players have a misconception that they need to labor through their practices, grind away, and hate every minute in order to improve; they believe in the "No pain, no gain" illusion. Foolishly, they believe that, only when they have achieved their developmental goals, then and only then should they allow themselves to enjoy the experience. This approach is completely backwards. It will stymie your development, at best, and, at worst, it could drive you to quit the game.

Please, don't misunderstand my point. I am not minimizing the importance of hard work. Quite the contrary: your capacity to work hard, learn, and improve corresponds to your level of enjoyment and passion for the game. When you look forward to playing, you will experience a profound relaxation, both physically and mentally. This in turn will enhance your intrinsic motivation—the inner drive that motivates you—to play the game and achieve your goals. It will enable you to continue to enjoy the game even while you endure some difficult moments in taking your game to the next level. Don't confuse having fun and enjoyment with having a laissez-faire attitude toward work or with lacking the "killer instinct" to win matches. The opposite is true: enjoying your time on the court is one of the keys to being a great competitor.

Learning to appreciate the joy of playing the game is the foundation from which you can truly develop into the best player you can be. World-class professionals understand this. Now it is time for you to buy into it as well. So, if you are not having fun playing tennis—this is the first and most important issue in your game that needs to be addressed. You cannot catapult your game to the next level unless you learn this lesson.

The Big Question

Now the big question: How can you ensure that you are deriving fun and enjoyment each time you step out on the court? Four quick and simple steps will help you determine this:

1. Be aware of the most common pitfalls to having fun and enjoyment (see table 10.1, pages 180–183).

2. Know which simple, yet powerful, things you can do to enhance the pleasure you get from the game.

3. Do a self-evaluation to determine your personal likes and dislikes about practice and competition.

4. Make the necessary adjustments to your practices and competition in order to get more pleasure out of your game.

Self-Evaluation

Take the time to examine your personal experiences in tennis, and ask yourself two questions: "What gives me the most joy in my tennis?" and "What are the things that most negatively impact my love for the game?" For example, you may really enjoy playing a set of singles, or you may love working out with your friends. Those would be fun enhancers for you. Conversely, you may hate doing repetitive, extensive drilling or dislike playing mixed doubles. Those are obviously fun busters for you. Check out the fun enhancers and fun busters, listed in table 10.1, and rate each one for you, from 1 to 10, using form 10.1 (page 185). In addition, write in the space provided anything that may have been left out that truly impacts your enjoyment of tennis.

After you have completed the form, make adjustments in your training regimen and playing schedule to maximize the areas you enjoy and minimize the aspects that you dislike. For example, let's say your number-one personal fun buster is drilling on your weaknesses. Try focusing more on practicing your weapons. Though you shouldn't ignore your weaknesses, you can spend less (but more concentrated) time working on areas that you need to improve. If losing matches is a downer for you, schedule some matches against players whom you have a good chance to defeat. By being aware of what excites and motivates you and what turns you off, you can tailor your tennis experiences for maximum enjoyment and results.

TABLE 10.1

	Fun Busters vs. Fun Enhancers	
	Fun busters	**Fun enhancers**
Style	*Playing the wrong style—* Playing a style of game that goes against your personality is a sure way to spoil your enjoyment of tennis.	*Playing the right style—*Playing a style of game that is complementary to your personality is one of the most enjoyable aspects of tennis.
Perspective	*Losing perspective—*Trouble starts when you forget that tennis is first and foremost a game—intended to be fun! Even if you are the most serious player in the world, the game must never cease to be enjoyable.	*Remember to smile—*Tennis is a game and it's meant to be fun! Smile, enjoy the moment. Your game will thank you.
Technique	*Overloading on technique—* Too much emphasis on technique and how to do things kills spontaneity and flow and ultimately will kill your ability to learn how to play the game. Coaches often call this "paralysis by analysis." At best, you will learn how to hit the ball, but you will not learn how to compete and enjoy playing the game. Technique is not an end in itself; it is a facilitator in playing the game.	*Practice your strengths and your weaknesses—*Practice your strengths, which are the foundation of your confidence, but practice your weaknesses, too. It's really fun to have the consistent success that comes from practicing the things you do best. Besides, if you lose your weapons from not enough work, you will be in trouble.
Company	*Hanging out with the wrong crowd—*Playing or hanging out with people who bring you down is the fast track to discouragement. Stay away from people who complain about their	*Choose good company—* People who are positive, upbeat, and passionate about tennis rub off on you, helping make you enjoy yourself on the court, as well. Try to hang out with

TABLE 10.1

	Fun busters	Fun enhancers
	game, the courts, and the playing conditions; make derogatory comments; joke about their game and yours; or who are always negative and never seem to have fun on the court.	people who enjoy themselves on the court, and it will have a positive impact on your game, too.
Analysis	*Overanalyzing*—Analyzing everything you do on the court can rob you of spontaneity and take the joy out of playing. It can also lead to "paralysis by analysis."	*Start positive*—Always start your analysis of practice sessions or matches with what you did well. It is important to start out every time with a positive reinforcement that will encourage you to work hard and continue to improve. Only after identifying the positives in your performance should you focus on what you need to work on or what you need to improve.
Competition	*Practicing too much*—It can be depressing to practice day after day without having anything to work toward.	*Anticipate the competition*—Having some form of competition to look forward to, whether it's a club match or a tournament, will be a positive source of positive feedback and enjoyment. No one can practice and train without anticipating the reward of using what you learn in competition. It also gives you a specific goal to point toward in your practices.
Drilling	*Drilling yourself silly*—Doing a disproportionate amount of drilling in your practices	*Drill with a purpose*—If you want to enjoy a drilling session have a clear purpose

(continued on next page)

TABLE 10.1 *(continued from previous page)*

	Fun busters	Fun enhancers
	is a common mistake. Drilling can be fun and it is necessary some of the time. However, doing it to excess can be downright depressing! A major problem is that many drills are executed incorrectly. Learn how to drill effectively and keep it fun and interesting at the same time.	in mind, keep the sessions moving by adding variety, and don't drill for extended periods.
Winning	*Winning at all costs—* Everyone wants to win. However, an overemphasis on results creates a double-whammy. It destroys the joy of the game and, ironically, keeps you from achieving the results you are capable of achieving. Although you compete against an opponent, one of the secrets to success is realizing you are really out there challenging yourself.	*Plan for battle—*Knowing that you have an important match or a big tournament coming up can be a stressful situation, but the best players understand how to plan for such events. Learn to relish the challenge. Your mental approach to competition will go a long way toward determining your enjoyment and passion for the game. With the correct approach you will not only win more frequently, but you will relish the opportunity to compete.
Negativism	*Dwelling on your mistakes—* You can't dwell on mistakes or poor performances and still keep a high level of enjoyment. Stop the self-flagellation and get on with the match.	*Appreciate yourself—*Take time to appreciate your successes and performances. Know when you have played a good point or shot, even if you are on the losing end. It will build your self-confidence and increase your enjoyment of the game.

TABLE 10.1

	Fun busters	Fun enhancers
Improvement	*Never improving*—It is no fun to have a problem or deficiency in your game, work on it daily, and not see any improvement. Seek help from your DTL, a USPTA or PTR tennis professional.	*Plan to improve*—When you have a plan for how you are going to improve, it gives you focus, purpose, and positive anticipation. Having a clear developmental plan will not only increase your chances of improving, you'll find yourself even more excited to get to the courts and practice.
Practice	*Mindless practice*—Having no plan on how to practice, what to practice, or how often to practice leads to a lack of improvement and enjoyment.	*Practice with purpose*—Having a purpose for your practice sessions will give you the motivation to get to the courts and accomplish your goals.
Balance	*Never winning or never losing*—Consistently playing players who are out of your league, either better or worse than you, is a foolish proposition. This often happens in junior tennis with overzealous parents who play their children at too high or too low a level. An adult tennis player should be winning approximately 50 percent of the time. If you are a developing junior, roughly a 2-1 win-loss ratio is ideal.	*Push yourself to the limit*—It can be satisfying and exhilarating to have your skills truly tested by the challenge at hand. Whether you are facing an opponent in competition who pushes you to the limit or simply practicing a drill that demands all of your physical and mental effort, it will feel good to push yourself to the limit.

If you are serious about taking your game to the next level, you have to recognize that not everything you do in tennis always will be fun. It will be necessary for you to practice certain aspects of your game or in a particular manner that may not be all that enjoyable. But those instances will be few and far between. The key is to make the most out of any situation you are in. Remember, having fun and cultivating a passion for the game is the most important principle of this book. Keep that in mind every time you walk on the court—whether you are practicing at your local club or playing center court at the U.S. Open. Have fun and enjoy the experience! Enjoyment truly is the foundation from which to improve and play to your full potential.

Personal fun enhancers	Personal fun busters
1.	1.
2.	2.
3.	3.
4.	4.
5.	5.
6.	6.
7.	7.
8.	8.
9.	9.
10.	10.
Others:	Others:

Epilogue

I hope you have enjoyed the book and found it to be helpful to your tennis game. The 10 concepts I present are the keys to unlocking your full potential as a player. If you apply *any* of these concepts, it will improve your game. However, if you follow the steps I have laid out in each chapter in sequential order, from visualizing the player you'd ultimately like to become to developing a plan and preparing yourself for competition with match-like practices, you will see a profound improvement in your level of play.

For those of you who have children playing competitively or if you are a coach of young players, teaching these concepts will not only help their game but also, more importantly, it teaches them invaluable lessons about how to be successful in any endeavor they choose to pursue.

Remember—have fun, practice smart, and play hard. Tennis is truly a game for a lifetime.

Bibliography

1. Brody, H. 1987. *Tennis science for tennis players.* Philadelphia: University of Pennsylvania Press.

2. Covey, S. 1990. *Seven habits of highly effective people.* New York: Simon & Schuster.

3. Crespo, M., and D. Miley. 1998. *Advanced coaches manual.* London, England: International Tennis Federation.

4. Elliot, B., and R. Kilderry. 1983. *The art and science of tennis.* New York: Saunders.

5. Gould, D., K. Dieffenback, and A. Moffett. December 2001. *The development of psychological talent in US Olympic champions.*

6. Martens, R., and B. Sharkey. 1990. *Successful coaching.* Champaign, IL: Human Kinetics.

7. Martens, R. 1987. *Coaches guide to sport psychology.* Champaign, IL: Human Kinetics.

8. Roetert, P. *High performance coaching newsletter.* United States Tennis Association.

9. Schonborn, R. 1998. *Advanced techniques for competitive tennis.* Lansing, Michigan: Meyer & Meyer Verlag, Aachen Olten.

10. United States Tennis Assocation. 2000. *USA tennis high performance coaches guide.*

Index

About the Author

Nick Saviano is the director of coaching education for the United States Tennis Association (USTA) and is considered one of the leading tennis coaching educators in the world today. He is an internationally recognized developmental coach, having worked with and developed many players who have gone on to become some of the best in the world. He is a highly sought after public speaker and has presented at tennis coaching conventions throughout the world.

A world-class professional for nine years, Saviano achieved ranking in the top 50 in singles and has had wins over numerous top 10 players. His positions within the USTA have included National Coach and Director of Men's Tennis. He is a master professional with the United States Professional Tennis Association (USPTA) and was named Touring Coach of the Year in 1993, and a Professional Tennis Registry (PTR) member.

Saviano has written for many major publications on all aspects of the game, including *Tennis* magazine. He is also an editor for the *USTA High Performance Coaching Newsletter* which goes out to approximately 25,000 coaches quarterly. He resides in Davie, Florida, with his wife Jenny, and three daughters, Nicole, Amanda, and Jennifer.

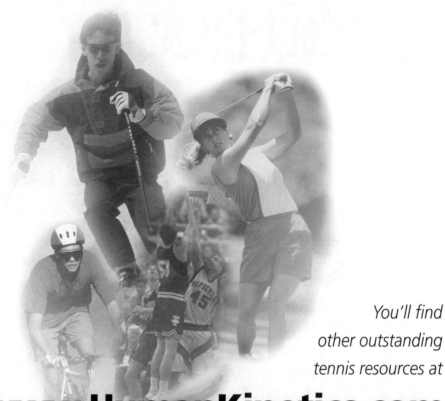